Practical Tinker Board

Getting Started and Building Projects with the ASUS Single-Board Computer

Liz Clark

Apress®

Practical Tinker Board: Getting Started and Building Projects with the ASUS Single-Board Computer

Liz Clark
Boston, MA, USA

ISBN-13 (pbk): 978-1-4842-3825-7   ISBN-13 (electronic): 978-1-4842-3826-4
https://doi.org/10.1007/978-1-4842-3826-4

Library of Congress Control Number: 2018965217

Copyright © 2019 by Liz Clark

Managing Director, Apress Media LLC: Welmoed Spahr
Acquisitions Editor: Natalie Pao
Development Editor: James Markham
Coordinating Editor: Jessica Vakili

Cover image designed by Freepik (www.freepik.com)

Distributed to the book trade worldwide by Springer Science+Business Media New York, 233 Spring Street, 6th Floor, New York, NY 10013. Phone 1-800-SPRINGER, fax (201) 348-4505, e-mail orders-ny@springer-sbm.com, or visit www.springeronline.com. Apress Media, LLC is a California LLC and the sole member (owner) is Springer Science + Business Media Finance Inc (SSBM Finance Inc). SSBM Finance Inc is a **Delaware** corporation.

For information on translations, please e-mail rights@apress.com, or visit http://www.apress.com/rights-permissions.

Apress titles may be purchased in bulk for academic, corporate, or promotional use. eBook versions and licenses are also available for most titles. For more information, reference our Print and eBook Bulk Sales web page at http://www.apress.com/bulk-sales.

Any source code or other supplementary material referenced by the author in this book is available to readers on GitHub via the book's product page, located at www.apress.com/978-1-4842-3825-7. For more detailed information, please visit http://www.apress.com/source-code.

Printed on acid-free paper

*This book is dedicated to my mom, Linda,
for always believing in me and for being an amazing
teacher, both inside and outside the classroom.*

Table of Contents

About the Author

Liz Clark has been creating and working with technology her entire life. Always wanting to learn more, she began a YouTube channel after college called Blitz City DIY to document and share her projects with the hopes of inspiring others to explore electronics, open source and all things DIY. When she isn't coding or soldering a circuit, she can usually be found either playing guitar or hanging out with her two cats, who often make cameos in her work.

Introduction

The goal of Practical Tinker Board is just what the title implies: to provide a realistic guide showing how to best approach and use the Tinker Board single-board computer.

The approach that I took when writing this book was to ask myself what I wish I had known when I was getting started with the Tinker Board, from features to limitations in both software and hardware. As a result, this book contains introductions to many concepts that aren't exclusive to the Tinker Board, because exploring a single-board computer is not a singly focused pursuit; it pulls from many concepts in the realms of open source development and electronics.

After reading this book and following along with the tutorials and projects, you'll have the skills and tools to go forward and create your own projects with the platform. It isn't meant to be an all-encompassing encyclopedia, just to guide you to a point of independence using the Tinker Board. This book also attempts to ease some of the frustrations that often come with using a brand-new piece of hardware. I hope that it helps beginners by making those first steps more accessible and that it provides inspiration for more experienced users. Platforms like the Tinker Board hold so many possibilities that are only limited by the user's imagination and skills. May this book be a resource to help you achieve your goals.

PART I

Getting Started

CHAPTER 1

What is the ASUS Tinker Board?

Before diving in, let's discuss some basics. What is a single-board computer? What can it do? And why would you want to use one in a project?

A Little Context

The maker movement has empowered the everyday person to tap into an intrinsic human element: making things. The ability to create robots or weather stations or other large-scale intelligent devices was once reserved for the most educated among us, with access to expensive equipment and fabrication tools. Now most of these items and skill sets can be acquired by anyone with a modest budget who just has the urge to learn. But as the abilities and interests of makers grow, the power and versatility of the resources must grow as well.

The Tinker Board is a part of the next wave of more powerful maker tools. As a single-board computer, it offers a multitude of options for a maker. It can control hardware with code, it can run specialized operating systems for niche projects, or it can be a small–form-factor computer for personal use.

© Liz Clark 2019
L. Clark, *Practical Tinker Board*, https://doi.org/10.1007/978-1-4842-3826-4_1

What Is a Single-Board Computer?

But let's back up for a moment. What exactly is a single-board computer?
A single-board computer (SBC) has a fairly self-explanatory name. It's
a computer that has all of its components fit onto one circuit board that
usually fits in the palm of your hand. Most desktop computers have a
motherboard with modules that plug in, including the CPU, RAM, graphics
card, and so on. By contrast, an SBC usually has everything soldered
directly to the board so that the user just needs to provide power and
peripherals to be up and running.

System on a Chip

A hallmark of SBCs is that they usually feature a system on a chip (SoC).
An SoC is an integrated circuit (IC) that contains most of the main
components of a computer in one package that takes up a single spot on a
circuit board. The processor is often an Advanced RISC Machine (ARM)-
based architecture, which is also found in modern Android phones and
Chromebooks.

The power and technology found inside modern consumer devices
in an unlocked form factor available to makers has a lot of possibilities.
Makers can expand on their project's limits without breaking the bank,
which leads us back to the Tinker Board.

The Tinker Board's Hardware

The Tinker Board, illustrated in Figure 1-1, is a lot like other SBCs and
does have its own SoC; specifically, a Rockchip RK3288. The RK3288's
processor is an ARM Cortex-A17, which has four cores clocked at 1.8GHz.
Of course, more experienced users can try overclocking the chip at their
own risk.

Figure 1-1. *The ASUS Tinker Board*

Its GPU is an ARM Mali-T760, which also has four cores and is clocked at 600MHz. For RAM, it has 2GB of LPDDR3 memory, which gives a nice amount of headroom to avoid bottlenecking with the processor and GPU specs.

For inputs and outputs (I/O), as shown in Figure 1-2, it features four USB 2.0 ports to connect peripherals and HID devices. There is also an Ethernet jack for a wired Internet connection. However, the board also has Wi-Fi capabilities if you need it to be mobile. It takes power through a micro-USB connection but requires a relatively large power supply of at least 5V/2A-2.5A for the original Tinker Board and 5V/3A for the Tinker Board S, which is a consequence of the hefty RK3288.

HDMI 1.4 is available on the board for video at 1080p and 4K for some applications. It can also carry audio, but if you prefer a dedicated audio output there is a 3.5mm headphone jack that can play up to 24-bit/192KHz resolution.

For storage, like other SBCs, the Tinker Board offers a microSD card slot to run the OS and native files. Of course, if you find you need expanded storage you can take advantage of the previously mentioned USB 2.0 ports.

Figure 1-2. *The Tinker Board's four USB 2.0 ports and Ethernet port*

GPIO

One of the Tinker Board's most prominent and unique features, though, is the set of general purpose input/output (GPIO) pins. The GPIO pins are breakout pins that allow external electronic components and circuits to interact with the Tinker Board.

This enables the Tinker Board to go beyond just a small circuit board with the same features as your average PC. By having access to the GPIO, you can build circuits using a variety of components to create unique projects that you have full control over.

There are 40 individual pins arranged in two horizontal rows of 20 (Figure 1-3). Each pin is identified by a number, and the Tinker Board has the GPIO header color-coded so that you can easily tell at a glance what a pin's dedicated function is.

A plus for the Tinker Board is that it shares a GPIO pinout with the Raspberry Pi series of SBCs. This means that existing circuits for the Raspberry Pi can, in most cases, be ported to the Tinker Board with no problems.

There are also add-on modules for the Raspberry Pi series of boards, called HATs and Bonnets. These add-ons have a female port that fits directly onto the GPIO pins and have pre-built circuits for more complicated applications, such as servo motor control, LED matrixes, camera control, and so on. Since the Tinker Board has an identical pinout, these add-ons can in many cases work with the Tinker Board in many cases.

You can use a variety of coding languages to interact with hardware connected via the GPIO pins. Python and C are very popular choices and have many open source libraries available. In a later chapter, we'll go in-depth on the process of developing hardware control applications and build some basic circuits to test features. Most of the projects featured in this book will also take advantage of the GPIO pins.

Figure 1-3. A closer look at the Tinker Board's GPIO pins. Note that they are color-coded to easily identify their individual functions.

Tinker Board S

The newest update to the Tinker Board family is the Tinker Board S. On the surface, the Tinker Board S looks very much the same as the original Tinker Board. However, there are some key differences that could make a big difference in performance for some projects and use cases.

eMMC

The most notable addition to the Tinker Board S is the inclusion of 16GB of on-board eMMC (embedded MultiMediaCard) flash storage. The advantage of eMMC is that since it's soldered directly to the board, it doesn't utilize a lot of RAM; it can communicate small pieces of data between the other onboard components more easily than external storage.

The speeds are similar to what you'll experience with an SD card, which is why you'll see the biggest advantage with small pieces of data. But when you are working on a project that is pushing the hardware to its limit, on-board eMMC can make a big difference for running your operating system. We'll discuss the different storage methods and what you'll need in the next chapter.

I2S

Looking toward the GPIO, the designers made a significant change to the I2S (inter-IC sound) functionality on the Tinker Board S. As the name suggests, I2S allows sound in the form of PCM audio data to be transmitted between integrated circuits by separating the clock and serial data into separate channels. This is ideal for high-stakes audio applications when dealing with digital systems and is used with DACs (digital-to-analog converters) for high-quality audiophile listening experiences.

Traditionally, the clock speed for I2S can act in either master mode, where the pin's output sets the clock, or slave mode, where the pin accepts the clock from an external source. The original Tinker Board's I2S pins only allowed it to act in master mode, but for the Tinker Board S, the pins can act in either master or slave mode. This gives greater flexibility for audio projects with the Tinker Board S and will allow it to have more compatibility with specialty DACs and ADCs. There are DAC and ADC hats available that fit over the GPIO pins. We'll be looking at these along with a specialized audio operating system in a project later in this book.

An additional audio upgrade on the Tinker Board S is the ability for the board to automatically switch between the 3.5mm jack and HDMI for audio output once a source is plugged in. This will be incredibly helpful for a traditional desktop setup or a home media center project.

Power-on Header

The final update for the Tinker Board S is the addition of a two-pin power-on header. This may seem trivial, but one of the biggest features missing from many single-board computers is the ability to turn the board on discretely. The original Tinker Board, along with many others, can only be turned on by plugging the power supply into the board.

Makers have shared mods that use the GPIO to hook-up a power button, but that sacrifices valuable GPIO pins for a very simple function. Having dedicated pins that are separate from the GPIO on the Tinker Board S for this purpose is very useful and simple for users who want the ability to embed their board in a housing or avoid having to repeatedly unplug and plug in their board.

Original Tinker Board or Tinker Board S?

Aside from these changes, the Tinker Board S is very much the same as the original Tinker Board. It uses the same SoC, GPU, RAM, I/O, GPIO (apart from the updated I2S feature) and form factor. Most users may not even notice the differences between these two boards since the updates to the Tinker Board S are specialized in nature.

However, these updates can also be the difference between a smooth project experience and a frustrating one. When choosing between the two, it's important to consider your use case scenario and make your decision from there. Both boards will be referenced throughout this book to demonstrate if one has an advantage over the other for certain tasks. This should help you in your decision when planning your projects.

Conclusion

It's these features and abilities that bring projects to the next level with the Tinker Board and similar SBCs. Compared to a more basic platform, like the Arduino Uno board, the possibilities expand when it comes to the different peripherals and technologies that you can seamlessly incorporate. For example, providing an Arduino-based project with Internet connectivity is possible, but getting the board online is almost a project by itself. With the Tinker Board, Wi-Fi is already a built-in feature for the board so it's as simple as signing into your network or plugging in an Ethernet cable.

The one thing that could hold the Tinker Board back is the fact that the RK3288 is running on the ARMv7-A architecture, which is 32-bit rather than the more modern 64-bit. However, most SBC operating systems and processes do not utilize 64-bit at this time, so you shouldn't experience issues with your projects. It's just something to keep in mind about the architecture of the hardware.

The RK3288 is built to streamline heavier processes since it has hardware acceleration for larger video files and codecs, which is often a performance choke point for SBCs. It's also been used in many Android phones and Chromebooks; this shows that it can stand-up to everyday use, which is a good vote of confidence for its use in an SBC.

This brings us to a question that you may have asked yourself already: why use the Tinker Board over another SBC where there are so many to choose from? Since the Tinker Board has higher specs than the average SBC, it's perfect for more advanced projects that would have pushed the limits of other SBCs in the past. It's also a great choice for makers or tech enthusiasts who want to dig a bit deeper into different Linux distributions.

So if you're curious about exploring Linux further and building projects that push the boundaries, then the Tinker Board is a good choice for you. In Chapter 2 let's discuss what peripherals you need to take full advantage of the Tinker Board's features.

Ready to Begin: What Do You Need to Use a Tinker Board?

We're almost ready to dive into using the Tinker Board. But before we do that, we need to go over a few very important accessories that will allow you to have a successful experience.

What Do You Need?

As mentioned in the previous chapter, single-board computers arrive with all components installed, so no additional computer hardware modules are needed, besides storage. However, other vital accessories are needed in order to use the Tinker Board properly.

Cooling

The first, and one of the most important, is included in the box. It's the heat sink for the SoC processor. For the processor to operate properly, a heat sink needs to be installed. The heat sink included with the Tinker Board is a good size and will offer proper cooling for everyday use. This method of cooling is called passive cooling, since heat is being expelled without an active force directly applied, such as air or water.

© Liz Clark 2019
L. Clark, *Practical Tinker Board*, https://doi.org/10.1007/978-1-4842-3826-4_2

You may have used other single-board computers in the past without a heat sink. For lower-powered boards, that is usually fine. However, as mentioned in the first chapter, the Tinker Board is more powerful than many other single-board computers; it has an SoC that is found in consumer products such as Android phones and Chromebooks. With an SoC of this power, a heat sink is not optional. Without it, you may experience thermal throttling, which occurs when a processor cannot perform to its full potential because of overheating. If it operates in this state for too long, it may even damage the SoC and make the board inoperable. It's the electronics equivalent of not giving a plant any water. So please, cool your board responsibly.

Installing the heat sink is simple. On the back is a thermal pad with a sheet of protective plastic. Simply peel off the plastic and stick the thermal pad to the processor. Apply some pressure to ensure good contact between the thermal pad and the processor. After this, the heat sink should be firmly attached to the Tinker Board as shown in Figure 2-1.

If for any reason you ever need to remove the heat sink, replacement thermal pads can be purchased in sheets and then cut to fit the processor die size. You may find over time with heavy usage that this will need to be done to maintain proper temperatures, similar to changing thermal paste on a desktop computer's CPU.

Figure 2-1. *An overhead view of the installed heat sink that is included with the Tinker Board*

Other Cooling Methods

Of course, you aren't limited to this stock heat sink. You can also investigate other, aftermarket heat sinks, if they fit the die size of the processor. This could be helpful in various ways. For example, you could install a shorter heat sink to fit into a housing for a project or a larger heat sink if you know that your project will need better cooling than the stock heat sink can provide. Aesthetics can also motivate a heat sink swap if this will be a visible component in your project and you're going for a certain look.

Heat sinks can also be applied to other ICs on the board, such as the GPU or even RAM if you want to ensure optimal cooling and performance for high-demand projects. The process for applying a heat sink to these ICs would be the same as applying one to the processor. You would just need a thermal pad and heat sink that fit the die size.

Your cooling options aren't limited to just heat sinks, though. You can also attach a small fan, either with a mounting kit or in a case, to a heat sink so that the processor can be actively cooled rather than just passively. This creates a cooling solution similar to desktop PCs that often have a fan and heat sink mounted together over the CPU.

This solution is especially effective when the Tinker Board is in an enclosed housing with minimal natural airflow. You may also want to further emulate a desktop PC's cooling by having enclosure fans bringing air in and expelling it out through vents. By including fans inside the case, you could also keep the board passively cooled without a dedicated fan attached to the processor's heat sink.

A more intensive method would be to cool the board with water cooling techniques. This approach is definitely for enthusiasts, and it's uncertain whether a board of this size and power would really benefit from such an extreme cooling solution, but for an enthusiast who wants optimal temperatures it could be an interesting project.

For this technique, you would need a water block that fits onto the processor's die, as an aftermarket heat sink must, and then a pump and tubing to carry the water. Distilled water is often chosen for water cooling, but specialty fluids are also sold. There are examples of makers implementing this with single-board computers, but again it's unclear that the effort and cost associated with water cooling are viable for a piece of hardware like the Tinker Board. There is also the additional risk of a leak with water cooling, but it would be up to you whether the risk was worth it for the possible reward of optimal temperatures combined with the aesthetic and accomplishment of water cooling.

Note   Using a cooling solution outside the heat sink provided by ASUS for the Tinker Board could result in undesired effects or performance. It's important to do your research for your specific cooling need before installing an aftermarket solution.

Power

Once your cooling solution is installed, you're getting closer to using the Tinker Board. But you can't really use the Tinker Board without it being turned on, can you? For this, of course, you'll need a power supply. Power can be delivered to the Tinker Board in two ways. The first, which is the most common and easiest, is through the micro-USB power port with a micro-USB power supply. It's important to make sure that your power supply is rated at 5V/2A-2.5A for the original Tinker Board and 5V/3A for the Tinker Board S. ASUS recommends a linear power supply, but people have had success with switching power supplies as well.

It's important to use a properly rated power supply to ensure that the Tinker Board operates as expected. It has a higher amperage requirement than many other single-board computers because of the power requirements for the RK3288. If you use a power supply that is rated lower than 2–2.5A, you may experience display issues, processing slowdowns, or issues with peripherals plugged into the USB ports. The Tinker Board S will not even boot with a power supply that has an amperage lower than 3A. On the other end of things, if you use a power supply with a voltage rating that is higher than 5V, you may short out the board, since it will be receiving a higher voltage than the components and circuitry are designed for.

Note   On the subject of power, if you're in a dry environment that can cause static discharge, please avoid touching the circuitry or ICs on the board without being grounded, as you can inadvertently short out a component and render it inoperable.

Advanced Power Option

For more advanced enthusiast users there is an additional option to power the Tinker Board—use the GPIO pins, which will bypass the on-board regulators. If this is done improperly, though, it can short out your board. However, this power method can be beneficial in certain situations and projects, since it provides a more direct power source that is unfiltered and as a result can allow the board to draw a more stable and slightly higher current. But the benefit to this method is also its detriment, since there is no over-voltage-protection like that found with the micro-USB power option. You are connecting power directly to the 5V line. But if you're feeling brave, you have the electrical experience, and you think you have a genuine use case for it, then you can proceed with caution.

Wiring

First, you'll need a steady and stable 5V power supply line with no more than 1A. This should come from a bench power supply or another trusted source. You'll be connecting the positive lead to pin 2 (5V) and then ground to pin 6 (GND) on the GPIO. Each 5V pin can only handle 1A since there is no filtering on these supply lines. If you need more than 1A available (which you probably will), then you'll need to connect to two 5V pins (pin 2 and pin 4) to have a combined amperage of 2A and two ground pins (pin 6 and pin 9). You can get away with using a single ground pin if necessary, but grounding both connections individually can add more stability to your connection.

Note   The Tinker Board's GPIO is color-coded to help in easily visually identifying the pins. The 5V pins are red and the ground pins are black, so this will help avoid any mistakes. We'll be going over the GPIO in more detail in a later chapter.

You'll more than likely stick with the original, suggested option of using a micro-USB power supply to power your Tinker Board, but it's always good to be aware of other methods available. One thing you'll immediately notice related to power is that the Tinker Board does not have a dedicated power button. It is only turned on when it receives power and can only be safely turned off via your chosen operating system. As previously discussed in Chapter 1, the new Tinker Board S does have the option to wire-up a dedicated power button with a power-on header separate from the GPIO. This is done by shorting the headers while power is connected to the board.

Peripherals

Power won't be the only connection that you'll have to make to fully utilize the Tinker Board. At least on first boot with TinkerOS, you'll need all of the peripherals that you'd normally need for a desktop computer. These include a keyboard, mouse, monitor, and possibly speakers.

Keyboard and Mouse Choice

For your keyboard and mouse choice, it's going to come down to personal preference. You'll utilize the USB ports to connect them and can choose either a wired or a wireless option. Wireless will give you a bit more flexibility and allow you to have more desk space if your work area is cramped, since you'll be able to have the keyboard and mouse farther away from the Tinker Board.

To further save space and USB ports, there are wireless keyboards that also include a mouse trackpad on the side. This configuration uses only one USB wireless receiver, which leaves you with three available USB ports rather than just two if a mouse and keyboard are used separately. A common option is the Logitech K410 (Figure 2-2) and other similar models, which are often used for HTPCs (home theater PCs). They have also become a favorite of single-board computer users because of their compact size and single USB port.

Figure 2-2. *The Logitech K410 wireless keyboard and mouse. Note the single wireless dongle plugged into the Tinker Board.*

Monitor and Speakers

Much like the keyboard and mouse choices, what you use for a monitor and speaker solution will be up to personal preference. The Tinker Board has an HDMI output, so a monitor that accepts HDMI would be ideal. Of course, an adapter can always be used if your monitor doesn't have HDMI as an option. There are many different types of monitors that can work with the Tinker Board, but it all depends on your setup.

If you're working at a desk, then a traditional desktop monitor should fit your needs, preferably with at least 1920×1080 resolution. If you aren't planning to have a dedicated workspace for your Tinker Board, you can also use your TV as a monitor. In fact, some projects may make sense to have attached to your TV; especially if they are media or file-based projects.

The Tinker Board can transmit audio through either the HDMI port or the 3.5mm jack, as shown in Figure 2-3. If your monitor has speakers, or if you're using a TV as your monitor, then you can utilize the HDMI audio. If you'd prefer to use portable speakers, then you'll use the 3.5mm jack and will need a 3.5mm cable to connect it. Depending on your operating system, you may need to configure your Tinker Board's audio output to fit your preference. As mentioned in Chapter 1, the Tinker Board S is able to switch between the 3.5mm jack and HDMI port by detecting when a cable is plugged in.

Figure 2-3. *The Tinker Board's HDMI port and 3.5mm audio jack. To the left of the HDMI port is the Micro USB port for power.*

Storage

The last add-on item that you'll need is storage to run an operating system. Most commonly, a microSD card is used for this purpose. There is an included microSD card slot on the back of the Tinker Board (Figure 2-4), and it is configured to look for bootable media there. The card's capacity should be at least 8GB for most operating systems. 16GB is your best bet, since it will allow enough capacity for the operating system and any files that you create or need to store without having to add-on additional USB storage. Of course, this will all be determined by your use case, but for the average scenario a 16GB card will be the most balanced solution.

Another option is to run the OS from a USB flash drive or hard drive. This can be useful if you're going to be using the Tinker Board as an everyday task machine and want all of your files on the same drive as your OS instead of splitting between an SD card and removable storage. This method still requires a microSD card, though, since the Tinker Board will look there for bootable media. A script needs to be loaded onto the card to tell the Tinker Board upon boot to use the USB device to boot. We'll go over preparing boot drives, including this method, in more detail in an upcoming chapter.

Figure 2-4. *The back of the Tinker Board. The microSD card slot is located on the left side.*

eMMC

As discussed in Chapter 1, the new Tinker Board S features an additional on-board option for bootable storage in the form of the 16GB eMMC flash. It has a speed similar to a microSD card on the Tinker Board, since they both utilize the same SD 3.0 speed controller. But because it's soldered to the board and has a direct connection, it has the benefit of being physically more stable than a removable SD card and in certain applications may be more desirable.

To load an OS onto the eMMC module, you'll need a micro-USB cable that is capable of transferring data. Plugging the board into your computer will allow the board to be recognized as a removable storage device. You can then load the bootable image onto the Tinker Board for it to be loaded onto the eMMC module. Again, we'll go over preparing bootable media in a later chapter.

Optional: Cases

One optional item that you may want for your Tinker Board is some sort of case or housing to protect it. The Tinker Board can certainly survive in the wild without any housing, but since it is a circuit board with exposed connections it would benefit from the extra safety precaution.

The options for how you can store your board are almost endless. This is another area where sharing the same form factor as the Raspberry Pi 3 comes in handy, since it means that most cases designed for the Pi can be used for the Tinker Board. The only incompatibility may occur with a case designed to have the processor and heat sink extend from the case, since the Tinker Board's processor die is larger than the Pi's. Otherwise, you should find success in cross compatibility.

Types of Cases

Cases are made from many materials. Popular choices include acrylic, plastic, and even metal or wood. For form factors, a classic snap-fit box is very common with cutouts for the different ports. These options are also usually very economical. There are also laser-cut cases that uses layers of acrylic or wood to build up a low-profile case. Some cases are made to emulate classic computer hardware or other pieces of technology. These cases are often more about aesthetics than function, but some do have some interesting features, such as power buttons or routing to have USB ports connect on a specific side of the case.

Incorporating similar features, a recent innovation has been small cases that resemble desktop computer cases. These often stand vertically like PC towers and have air vents, as well as fans and connectors to integrate power and other ports into extensions built into the case for a more compact desktop experience.

DIY options are also available. There are countless files available from makers who have designed their own cases for fabrication with a 3D printer or CNC machine. If you have an interest in either of these hobbies, then creating your own case with one of these methods may be a fun project for you.

Case choice is subjective, and as long as it fits your Tinker Board, then it's more than likely a good choice. Of course, if your project or application is going to be pushing the Tinker Board's limits and as a result creating a lot of heat, then it's important to think about airflow and cooling when considering a case. Some cases also enclose the GPIO pins; so if you're planning to have access to those, then you'll want to keep that in mind as well.

Conclusion

This may seem like a lot of accessories, especially considering the size of the Tinker Board. However, if you follow these guidelines you will set yourself up to have the most successful experience with the Tinker Board. Although it may be easy to cut corners on accessories to get up and running, it will more than likely come back to haunt you as you try more complicated projects or different operating systems. It's best to start off on the right foot so that when you do have to do some troubleshooting you can immediately rule out that you are using out of spec peripherals, storage or cooling solutions.

This concludes the introduction portion of this book. At this point you should have a good understanding of what is making the Tinker Board tick from a hardware perspective, and why a Tinker Board would be used for a project. You should also know what is required for accessories for the Tinker Board to avoid any issues. Now it's time for the fun stuff: actually using the Tinker Board! Let's move on to Part II and get to know TinkerOS, the GPIO pins, and Android on the Tinker Board.

CHAPTER 3

Installing an Operating System

In this chapter we're going to go over the process of preparing your storage device to install an operating system for your Tinker Board.

Now that you have all of your materials from Chapter 2 and you have a better idea of exactly how the Tinker Board works, it's time to get into the nitty-gritty aspects of working with the Tinker Board. To begin, we're going to prepare your chosen storage solution to install an operating system (OS) and then go through the steps to download your chosen operating system's disk image and install the OS on your storage device so that it can run on your Tinker Board.

Note Many users will utilize a microSD card for their operating system if they are using the original Tinker Board, or even the Tinker Board S, so the following instructions will assume that is the case. If you are using the eMMC flash on the Tinker Board S, the steps will be the same unless otherwise noted.

© Liz Clark 2019
L. Clark, *Practical Tinker Board*, https://doi.org/10.1007/978-1-4842-3826-4_3

Prepping the SD Card

The first step in loading an OS onto an SD card is to format the card so that it is ready to write the OS files without any glitches or data corruption. Formatting ensures that the storage does not have any remaining or proprietary files from previous use or from the factory. It's especially important to format properly when prepping storage for an operating system, since it will have a direct connection to the stability and long-term health of the OS.

How do you format storage, though? There are built-in utilities within your desktop operating system, whether you are on Windows, macOS, or Linux. For SD cards, the SD Association provides the SD Card Formatter program, which is a specialized program for a full and complete reformat. It's available for Windows and macOS, but not Linux. If you are on a Linux distribution, it may be worthwhile to run the SD Card Formatter in a Windows virtual machine (VM).

Note   If you are using the eMMC on the Tinker Board S, then you do not need to fully reformat it, since it has a built-in bootloader that would be deleted if fully reformatted.

It takes a lot longer to format the card using the software, but you will know that the card is fully cleared and ready to take on an OS. This process mainly comes in handy when you've had an OS installed on the card previously and want to do a fresh install or install a completely different OS.

Installing SD Card Formatter

The installation process for the SD Card Formatter program is very straightforward. You'll go to the SD Association's web site[1] and download the version for your desktop operating system, either macOS or Windows, and follow the installation instructions. Once the installation has completed, launch the program and select your SD card's drive letter from the drop-down menu as shown in Figure 3-1.

Figure 3-1. *The SD Association's SD Card Formatter software*

---

[1]https://www.sdcard.org/downloads/formatter_4/

Once you've selected your SD card, the program should also show the storage space available on the card. There is also an option at this point to label the drive, which will take effect after the formatting is finished. It's best practice to name the drive after the OS that you are going to load onto it; such as TinkerOS or Android.

Next, you'll select which type of format you want to proceed with. There are two options available, either quick format or overwrite format. For our purposes, we'll choose overwrite format to prep the card because it initializes the file system and does a more in-depth erasure process than the quick format option. You can read more about the exact parameters of the different formatting protocols in the SD Association's user manual[2] for the SD Card Formatter software.

Again, this process takes much longer than the quick format or your built-in utility within your desktop OS, but the time spent on the format will be worth it for the stability that your eventual OS will have.

Once you have your drive and format type selected, click Format. This begins the format process. A progress bar will appear so you can monitor the percentage that has completed. Once it finishes, you'll have a fully reformatted and blank SD card.

Downloading a Disk Image

There are many different operating systems available for the Tinker Board from the community and open source software projects. The first operating system that we're going to use for the Tinker Board, though, will come directly from ASUS. Specifically, we'll install TinkerOS, the Debian Linux distribution for the Tinker Board, and TinkerOS Android, an Android OS that will look familiar if you have an Android tablet or smart phone.

---

[2]https://www.sdcard.org/downloads/formatter_4/SD_CardFormatter5User
ManualEN_v0100.pdf

Note   The processes for downloading operating systems from other sources will be similar, but in this chapter we'll look specifically at the download processes for operating systems directly from ASUS; mainly TinkerOS. There will be specific information later in the book for other operating systems that are not from ASUS that we'll use for projects.

To download the ASUS operating systems, we'll go the ASUS web site for the Tinker Board,[3] as shown in Figure 3-2.

Figure 3-2. *The ASUS Tinker Board web site*

Here you'll click the Support tab at the top of the page. Once you reach the Support page, click the Driver and Tools tab. As shown in Figure 3-3, this will bring you to a page that says "Please select OS," with a drop-down menu. On the menu, select Others.

---

[3]https://www.asus.com/us/Single-Board-Computer/Tinker-Board/overview/

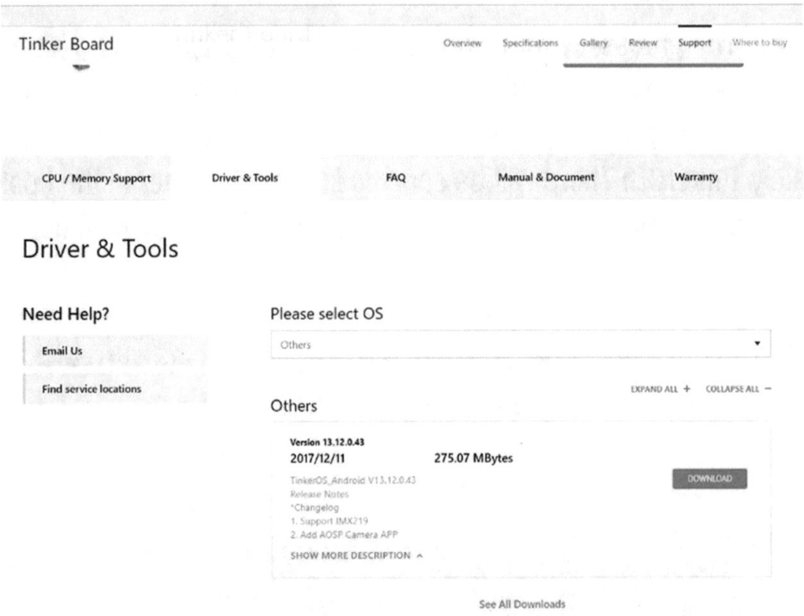

Figure 3-3. *The ASUS Tinker Board Support page with downloads*

The most recent downloadable release for the Tinker Board from
ASUS will appear at the top of the page. But if you click See All Downloads,
you'll be able to see all of the releases, past and present, for the Android
and TinkerOS distributions, as well as any additional software utilities or
resources; such as schematics and CAD drawings of the boards.

You will always want to download the most recent non-beta release for
the OS that you want to use. Of course, more experienced users may want
to experiment with beta releases to test certain features.

Note   Tinker Board S uses the same installations as the original
Tinker Board, beginning with TinkerOS version 2.0.4 and Android
version 13.12.0.43.

When you've decided on an OS, click the Download button to the right of the title. A zipped folder will begin downloading. Inside the folder is an .img file, which is the packaged disk image file that contains what will eventually become your OS for the Tinker Board. To access this file, you'll need to unzip the folder after the download finishes using your preferred utility and method.

Note   Not all disk images will be in the .img file format. Other formats, such as .iso, will work in the same way and are just different ways to package a disk image.

Writing an OS to Your Drive

The compressed disk image file can't be copied directly onto your storage media, though, because it can't be read by the Tinker Board in this format. It needs special software to write it to your drive so that it can be recognized and used by the Tinker Board.

To do this, we'll use Etcher. There are many different pieces of software that can accomplish this task, but Etcher has a lot going for it. It's open source, easy to use, and available for Windows, macOS, and Linux. You'll download and install it from its web site.[4]

Again, Etcher is incredibly simple to use; the process has only three steps. The first is to select the .img file that you just downloaded and unzipped. Click the Select Image button as shown in Figure 3-4, navigate to the unzipped folder with the .img file, and click to load it into Etcher.

---

[4]https://etcher.io/

Figure 3-4. *Etcher's GUI*

The next step is to select the drive that you want to use with your Tinker Board. This will be the SD card that you just formatted or other bootable media that has been prepped, such as the Tinker Board S itself to utilize the eMMC module.

When you select your drive, the label that you gave it during the formatting process may not show-up in Etcher. This is OK; just be sure to verify that it's the correct drive by identifying the drive letter. When you're sure that you've selected the correct disk image file and the correct drive, click "Flash!" and it will write the disk image onto the drive that you selected.

Note   This process erases everything that is on the selected drive; that is why it's very important to verify that you've selected the correct one. The fact that it erases the drive does not eliminate the need to properly format the drive, with the exception of eMMC, before this process.

Once the flashing process begins, Etcher will give you some information while it writes the image to your drive, as shown in Figure 3-5. It tells you the percentage complete, the estimated time left, and how quickly the drive is writing the data. The speed of your drive will depend on your computer's overall speed, how the drive is connected to your computer, and the actual speed that your drive is rated for.

Figure 3-5. *The information Etcher displays while it's flashing the OS to your drive*

When Etcher finishes, it will let you know that it is complete and ask if you want to flash the image again to another drive. If you don't need to do that, then you can exit Etcher and we can move on to booting the Tinker Board with your drive.

Note   Etcher's default setting is to eject the drive once the flashing process completes, so don't panic if you don't see your media after it finishes.

The First Boot

To boot up a new operating system with your Tinker Board for the first time, you'll slot in your SD card and then power on the board with your preferred power method. Of course, if you're using the eMMC module on the Tinker Board S, then you won't need to attach any storage.

The first boot for any OS will more than likely take a bit longer than normal, since file systems are being built and other settings are being configured. But as soon as you see the desktop pop-up, you'll know you've had a successful boot and it will finally be time to begin using your freshly installed operating system.

Booting from USB for TinkerOS

You currently have a ready-to-go OS installed and you could get started right now, but what about booting from a USB drive? This is currently possible for TinkerOS, so let's give it a try.

The procedure I'm about to describe was made possible by research and documentation from the community surrounding the Tinker Board. A full thread for the discussion of this topic can be found on the official Tinker Board Forum ("Install TinkerOS to HDD," 2017).[5] At this time, you'll still need to leave your imaged SD card (or eMMC for the Tinker Board S) mounted in the Tinker Board, since it is still seen as the boot device on a hardware level. Upon powering up, the SD card or eMMC will point to the USB device to boot and access the root partition after following these steps.

---

[5]The main discussion is found here: https://www.tinkerboarding.co.uk/forum/thread-73.html, which includes links to various resources.

Note   This discussion assumes that you have experience with Linux. If you don't, it's recommended that you boot from an SD card for now (or eMMC) and go on to the next chapter on TinkerOS, which will orient you to a Debian Linux desktop environment.

Prepping Your USB Device

First, you'll need to format your USB storage media, similar to the way you prepped the SD card or eMMC earlier. This erases everything on the drive, so be sure you've backed-up your files if your storage has been used before. When formatting your device, be sure to format it to exFAT formatting. Formatting your storage in this way will make things easier for your drive during the following steps.

Note   For USB storage, there isn't standardized formatting software as there is for SD cards. The best practice with this storage is to use your built-in formatting tool within your desktop's OS. But be sure to use a full format option rather than a quick or refresh format.

It's also important to note that your USB device should have at least the same capacity as your SD card. If you use a USB device that is smaller than your SD card, you will run into issues when copying the root partition. As discussed in Chapter 2, one of the main reasons you would want to boot from a USB device is for the increased storage capacity; so it's likely your USB storage is larger than your SD card, but that is something to keep in mind.

You'll also want to keep your USB device's speed in mind. If a drive is too slow, such as with an older mechanical drive, then you won't be able to boot from it because the files will not load fast enough for TinkerOS. It's recommended to use a flash-based USB device, such as a memory stick or SSD with a SATA to USB adapter cable.

There are a few ways to set up your TinkerOS install to boot from a USB device. The method we're going to use takes advantage of the built-in disk duplication tools in Linux and is done directly in the TinkerOS environment using terminal commands.

The Terminal

First, we're going to power-on the Tinker Board to boot into TinkerOS with the SD card or eMMC. You should find yourself in the desktop environment. Navigate to the terminal and open a new window. At this time, you should plug your freshly formatted and blank USB storage device into one of the USB ports.

Note   If you aren't sure where the terminal is, please reference the next chapter, which provides an orientation and walkthrough of TinkerOS.

Now that your USB device is plugged in, we need to see what disk name TinkerOS has given the USB device. To do this, we're going to enter `sudo fdisk -l` into the terminal. This lists all of the drives currently connected to the Tinker Board, as shown in Figure 3-6. More than likely, unless you have multiple drives connected to your Tinker Board, your USB device will show-up as `sda1,` and for this walkthrough we're going to assume that is the case. This will be important for the next steps. Also note that the SD card's root partition shows up as `mmcblk0p2`.

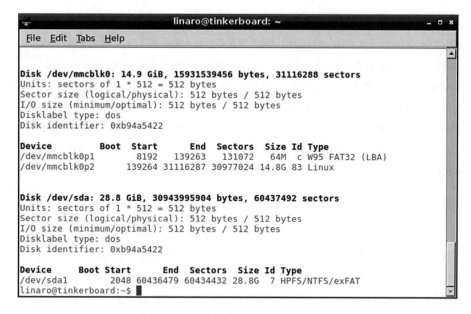

Figure 3-6. *The disk list provided by fdisk*

After confirming your drive names, it's time to start copying the files over to the USB device. To do this we're going to use the built-in dd (disk duplication) tool in Linux. This is a very powerful command and you can do even more with it than a simple duplication of data. However, because it is powerful and we're working with data, it's important to make sure you're typing everything in correctly and are sure that you're calling on the correct drives. The duplication command that we're going to use is this:

```
sudo dd if=/dev/mmcblk0p2 of=/dev/sda1 bs=512
```

This duplicates the root partition only, so that the root and file system configuration that was set up on the first boot with the SD card is now also present on the USB device along with the entire file system. This process can take a while, and it may appear that your terminal has frozen, but it's best to be patient and wait for the process to finish.

After the duplication has finished, we're going to force-check the USB storage device for errors using the fsck command e2fsck, since it is an ext4 disk. Traditionally, it's best to have this force-checking take place automatically on reboot, since running it while the system is up can have some risks. In this case, though, because we're transferring a boot drive it makes sense to run it now, since we can't move on with the boot migration until we know the disk is OK. The command to run in the terminal for this check is this:

```
sudo e2fsck -f /dev/sda1
```

After you've confirmed that the USB storage doesn't have any errors, it can be resized back to its full size. If you were to check its size right now, it would be identical to your SD card or eMMC's size because of how the partition was duplicated. Resizing is done using the resize2fs command from the same fsck family of commands that we just used to check the drive. The full command to run is

```
sudo resize2fs /dev/sda1
```

Once the resize has finished, we're going to install the nano text editor. This is a very important program in Debian Linux that lets you edit text files from the terminal, but it is not included in the default TinkerOS install from ASUS. To install it from the terminal, type

```
sudo apt-get install nano
```

After the installation completes, it's ready to use for the final, and most important, two steps in setting up the USB storage. We're going to be editing two text files that are used by TinkerOS to determine the boot device so that it knows to boot from the USB device.

The first file is extlinux.conf. To enter the text editor for this file, type sudo nano /boot/extlinux/extlinux.conf into the terminal. Once you're in the file, you'll need to add a piece of text to its last line.

Type `root=/dev/sda1` between `plymouth.ignore-serial-consoles` and `console=tty1` as shown in Figure 3-7. This targets the USB device as the root location. Save your changes by pressing Ctrl+X and saving before exiting. This will bring you back to the terminal. To verify that your changes were saved, you can type `sudo nano /boot/ext/extlinux.conf` into the terminal again to look at the file.

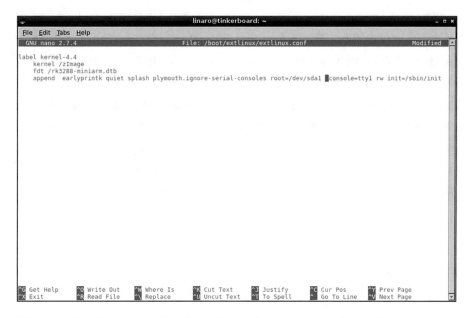

Figure 3-7. *How the edited version of extlinux.conf should appear*

The last file to edit is the `fstab` file. `fstab` is a configuration file that automatically mounts partitions. It also defines how the partitions are mounted. This is where we'll tell TinkerOS to mount the USB device as a boot drive. To do this, enter `sudo nano /etc/fstab` into the terminal to access the file through the text editor.

Once inside the file, you'll notice that there are very long strings of letters and numbers that have storage information to their right, such as boot designation and partition numbers. These are the SD card (or eMMC) and USB device's UUID numbers. UUID numbers are unique numbers assigned by the Linux operating system to identify removable devices. We can use the terminal to see exactly which UUID number corresponds to each drive so that we don't get confused.

Open a new terminal window and type

```
ls -l /dev/disk/by-uuid
```

This will list the drives with the more familiar labels that we've been referencing plus their UUID numbers. Now if we reference the fstab file at the same time, it makes a lot more sense as shown in Figure 3-8.

Turning our attention back to fstab, locate your SD Card's UUID number. Notice that /boot is typed to its right. Delete boot, leaving the /. You can also comment out this line using #. Next, find your USB device's UUID number and note that a / is also located to its right with no text. Type boot next to the / as shown in Figure 3-8. Save the file and return to the terminal.

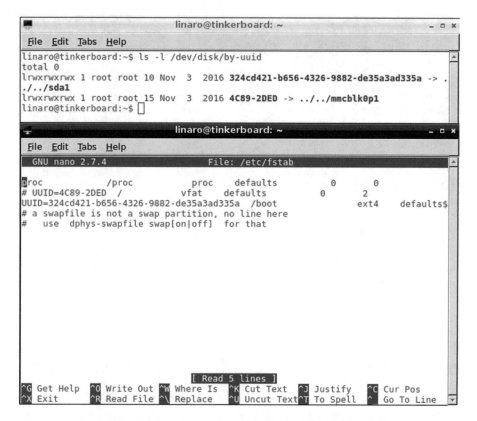

Figure 3-8. *The attached drive's UUID numbers side by side with the edited* fstab *file*

With that, all of the steps have been completed to boot from the USB device, but we should test things out first. In the terminal type sudo reboot to reboot the system. Do not remove either the SD card or the USB device. If you boot into the desktop environment successfully after the reboot, then things are looking good.

To check to see if TinkerOS is truly running from the USB device, navigate to the File Manager window and look at the free space in the bottom-right corner, as shown in Figure 3-9. If it shows the storage size of your USB device, then everything is truly set up and running properly.

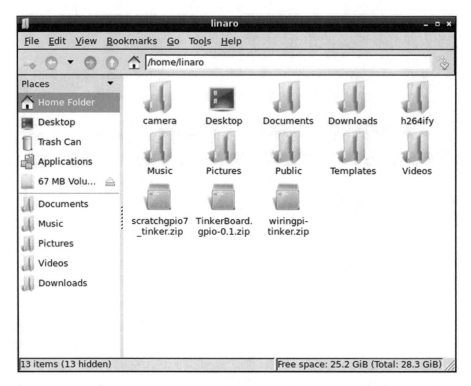

Figure 3-9. *The file system GUI. You can see the system's total space in the bottom-right corner to confirm that you are running TinkerOS on your USB device.*

Note If you receive a kernel panic or other error while doing that first reboot, it means that the Tinker Board can't find the proper boot device that you pointed it to by editing `extlinux.conf` and `fstab`. This can be fixed by taking your SD card, or Tinker Board S for eMMC, and plugging it into a different computer running a Linux OS to edit the two files back to their original configuration. After this, you should be able to boot properly from the card, or eMMC, to begin troubleshooting what went wrong.

Conclusion

By following these steps for formatting your storage, downloading a disk image, and flashing that image to your SD card or eMMC you have an OS ready to use with your Tinker Board. You may even be running TinkerOS from a USB device.

This chapter will be referred to throughout the book as we explore other operating systems. But now that we have an operating system ready to go, let's power up the Tinker Board and continue with our journey by looking in Chapter 4 at the Tinker Board's software provided by ASUS.

PART II

Official Operating Systems and GPIO

CHAPTER 4

Getting to Know TinkerOS

In this chapter we'll take a tour of TinkerOS, the Debian Linux distribution from ASUS for the Tinker Board.

Note   In the upcoming chapters it will be assumed that you are familiar with the concepts of commands and practices with the Linux terminal, such as sudo, apt-get, cmake, cd, and so on.

Finally, after a lot of preparation, you have everything you need to start using the Tinker Board with an operating system installed. The first OS we're going to tour is TinkerOS. Based on Debian Linux, it's maintained by ASUS and has a traditional desktop environment.

First Boot

If you have followed the disk imaging steps from the previous chapter, you may have already booted into the TinkerOS desktop by powering on the board with your chosen storage solution. Again, the first boot will take a bit longer than you might expect because of the file structures being installed.

© Liz Clark 2019
L. Clark, *Practical Tinker Board*, https://doi.org/10.1007/978-1-4842-3826-4_4

Once you get to the desktop, though, if you're new to Linux, you may notice that it looks a lot like a traditional Windows desktop with a task bar at the bottom of the screen and trash can icon for deleted files in the top left corner, as shown in Figure 4-1.

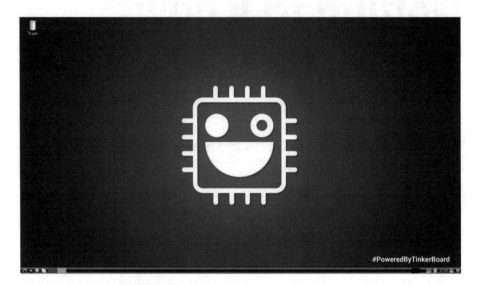

Figure 4-1. *The TinkerOS desktop*

What Is TinkerOS?

First, some background on TinkerOS. It is based on Debian Linux, and at the time this book is written utilizes Debian Stretch, which is Debian 9. Linux distributions also number their releases, similar to Windows and macOS. TinkerOS uses the LXDE desktop environment for Debian Stretch. There are a few different desktop environments available for Debian, and which one is best often comes down to personal preference. LXDE stands for lightweight desktop environment, and it definitely lives up to its name as it does not use a lot of resources and is fairly lightweight in its hardware utilization. Because of this, it makes a great choice for a single-board computer to run, leaving valuable hardware resources available for tasks.

The LXDE desktop environment is made-up of panels, which appear at the bottom of the desktop, in the area that would be called the task bar in Windows and macOS. These panels, controlled by the LXPanel utility, are completely customizable. As you become more comfortable with TinkerOS, you may want to change the default panel setup. We will go over how to do that shortly, but first let's take a quick tour of the default panel configuration for TinkerOS.

Getting Your Bearings

Starting at the bottom-left corner on the panel, you'll see the LXDE logo. When you click the icon, a menu will open, which resembles the Start menu in Windows and shows the preinstalled programs for TinkerOS. Don't worry; these programs are not bloatware. They're standard Linux programs, and in fact TinkerOS has fewer preinstalled programs than many other popular SBC Linux distributions, which may or may not be a good thing depending on your preferences.

The programs are sorted by category, as shown in Figure 4-2. At the top of the menu is the Accessories category, where you'll find things like a calculator, Leafpad (a low-level text editor), and similar utilities.

Figure 4-2. *The menu with categories for pre-installed programs*

Next is the Education category, where you'll find the programming language Scratch. If you aren't familiar with Scratch, it is a graphical programming language aimed at kids. But, if you're new to programming, you may find it helpful to understand how coding works. More experienced programmers may also find it to be a fun and quick way to test out a simple idea for a project. It can also offer a nice change of pace.

After Education is the Internet category. Here you'll find the default browser, which is Chromium, and the VNC Viewer. In case VNC (virtual network computing) Viewer is new to you, it's a standard program that allows you to connect remotely to a computer and control its GUI in a window on your desktop.

Following the Internet category is the Programming category. We'll be spending a lot of time here once we begin exploring the GPIO and working on projects. Here you'll find a few iterations of IDLE, which is a Python IDE we will try out later in the chapter, and again you'll find Scratch.

Up next is the Sound and Video category. Here is where you can adjust system settings for sound and utilize various media players for video and audio playback. We'll run some quick tests to make sure audio and video playback are working properly a bit later in this chapter.

After Sound and Video is the System Tools category. This category has some of your most valuable tools that you'll use in your day-to-day TinkerOS operations. These include the file manager, task manager, and most importantly the terminal. If you're new to Linux, the terminal will more than likely be your most-used program, since most tasks are completed with it by using commands.

The terminal is also what makes Linux such a useful operating system, since you can quickly accomplish complicated tasks with a little bit of text compared to a lot of clicking and attempting to navigate thru a GUI. It can seem intimidating at first, but after using it for a bit you'll find yourself automatically going to the terminal for tasks that you may have previously clicked around for.

The final category is Preferences, and it is quite large. As the name implies, here you'll find controls for many system settings, including but not limited to Bluetooth, monitor, keyboard and mouse, and power settings. If there's a setting you want to change for peripherals or how your board is operating, chances are you can come here and take care of it.

After Preferences are a few one-click utilities. Run allows you to quickly run a terminal command without having to go into a new terminal window, as shown in Figure 4-3, and Logout allows you to shut down, reboot, suspend your session, switch user, lock your screen, and log out. If you click this by mistake, you can get back to the desktop by clicking Cancel.

Figure 4-3. *The window for Run is helpful for quick command execution*

Other Panels

At the left of the panel, the icons to the right of the LXDE icon are shortcuts to individual programs, as shown in Figure 4-4. The first is a shortcut to the file manager. Next to that is a shortcut to Chromium, which as mentioned is the default web browser.

Figure 4-4. *The left-side panels*

If you aren't aware of Chromium, it is an open source browser developed and maintained by Google. You may have never used Linux before, but you more than likely have used the Google Chrome browser; and Chrome utilizes the source code of Chromium. Chromium as a result has a very similar feel to Chrome, but with fewer bells and whistles as it's designed to feel minimalistic. There are also features in Chrome, such as licensed media codecs and auto updates, that are not available in Chromium. Despite this, Chromium still provides a modern browser experience.

The next item is a shortcut to LXPanel, which as mentioned previously allows you to customize the panel options. We'll revisit this module shortly.

The final panel item on the left side of the desktop is the icon that lets you switch between desktops. The default setting is to be on desktop 1, but you can toggle between desktop 1 and 2 by clicking here. This allows you to have different setups for different tasks or to keep things from getting too cluttered when multitasking.

Moving over to the right of the screen, you'll see that the first item is a shortcut to the CPU Usage Monitor, as shown in Figure 4-5. This icon gives you a visual on your CPU's usage with a graph and can quickly tell you if you're bottlenecking your CPU if you happen to notice a slowdown in performance.

Figure 4-5. *The right- side panel*

Following the CPU Usage Monitor is the volume control. Left-clicking on the panel allows you to quickly adjust your system's overall volume or mute it. Right-clicking gives you a shortcut to volume control settings and a shortcut to get into the Mixer application for TinkerOS. Some of these items are also available under the Sound and Video category that we just looked at.

Next is your network information. Here you can see whether you have a network signal that is either wired via the Ethernet port on the Tinker Board or a Wi-Fi signal. You can also change your Wi-Fi information here and manage your VPN connections. We'll work on getting connected to Wi-Fi shortly.

After networking is a shortcut to Bluetooth settings, followed by the settings for date and time. Finally, you'll see shortcuts to lock the screen and log out.

Customizing Panels

As you can tell from our tour, the default panel configuration for TinkerOS is quite extensive and has a variety of shortcuts that will come in handy as you adjust to TinkerOS. It also has a similar aesthetic to a traditional Windows desktop, which you've more than likely used before. But what if you want a different look to your TinkerOS desktop? Or you have different programs that you'd prefer to have shortcuts for? Changes like these can all be made by customizing the panels.

To edit your panel preferences, right-click the Panel Settings panel to enter the Add/Remove Panel Items utility, as shown in Figure 4-6.

Figure 4-6. *Entering the Add/Remove Panel Items utility. Once it's opened, you can edit the way your TinkerOS desktop looks, from icons to desktop background.*

Once you're in the utility, you can change the geometry, location, and style of the panels along with selecting which programs are highlighted in the Panel Applets tab, as shown in Figure 4-7. It's a highly customizable feature of LXDE and other Linux desktops. Located next to this is the Appearance tab, where you can edit your desktop background and other display personalization details, such as the default font size.

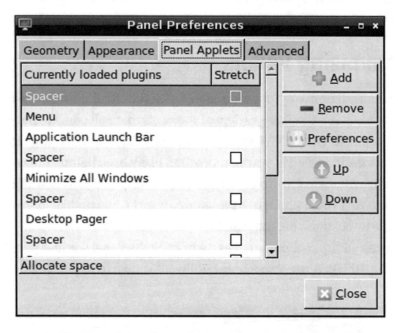

Figure 4-7. *The Panel Applets tab. Here you can choose the programs that you want to have panels and their location.*

For this walkthrough, we'll be utilizing the default layout for TinkerOS. However, feel free to experiment with your personal layout as you find your preferences or if you are an experienced Linux user.

Changing the Default Password

The first item that we should take care of with your fresh installation of TinkerOS is to change the default password, especially if you plan to connect your board to the Internet. The default username and password for the Tinker Board are "linaro" and "linaro", respectively. Of course, it isn't very secure to use the same word for both the username and password.

To change the password, navigate to Preferences ➤ Tinker Board Configuration. On the first tab, there's a button to Change Password as shown in Figure 4-8. Click it and then enter your new password. After saving, your new password is active.

Note   Make sure you write the password down in a safe spot. It would be a shame to get locked out of your TinkerOS installation.

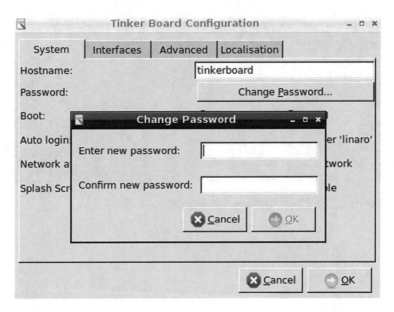

Figure 4-8. *Changing your password from the Tinker Board Configuration window. Make sure you write it down somewhere safe!*

Changing the Default Username

You can also change the default username as well if you want to have a more personalized experience in TinkerOS. You'll again navigate to Preferences, but this time, go to Users and Groups. There you'll see the default linaro profile. Here you can add other users and change settings as well. To change your username, click Change next to the name (Figure 4-9) and then type your desired username in the dialog box that pops up, as shown in Figure 4-10.

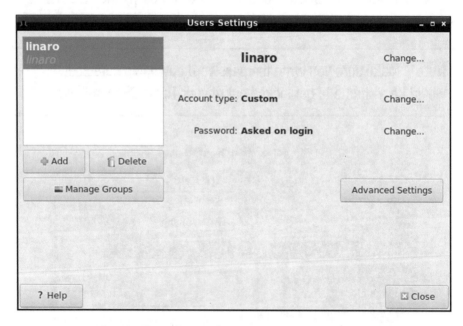

Figure 4-9. *The User Settings window*

Figure 4-10. *You can change the default username to anything you want*

You may have noticed that in the Tinker Board Configuration window where we changed the password, there was a box that had "auto login as linaro" checked off. You may be wondering if changing your username will mess with that setting. And no, luckily it does not. If you look at the Users Settings window (Figure 4-9), you'll see that "linaro" also appears in grayscale italic text underneath the username. This denotes the user group and is also the reason for a "custom" account type for the default user.

The option "auto login as linaro" refers to the user group linaro; not the username. So changing the default username does not mess up the login process or other things within the system. This has been an issue with previous SBCs, whose Linux systems and file hierarchies were set up to be dependent on a default system-defined username.

To test, you can try changing your username and doing a quick reboot. You should see that you aren't prompted to enter your password to get to the desktop. Of course, if you want to be prompted to enter your password to access the desktop, you can simply uncheck that auto login box.

Note   It isn't a necessity to change the default username, as that is more of an aesthetic or preferential change; but you should change your default password for security reasons, especially if you are connecting your board to the Internet.

And speaking of the Internet, let's get this board onto your Wi-Fi network.

Wi-Fi

After you've changed your password, let's connect to a Wi-Fi network. Although a wired connection is available via the Tinker Board's Ethernet jack, most will probably want to take advantage of the built-in wireless capability.

To connect to your chosen network, navigate to the Network panel on the task bar. Click on it and then select your network name from the list that appears, as shown in Figure 4-11. If you don't see your network in the initial listing, click the More Networks menu.

Figure 4-11. How Wi-Fi networks appear in TinkerOS

Note   If you have your network set up to be hidden, it obviously won't show up in the listing. Utilize the Connect to Hidden Wi-Fi Network option instead and enter your information as prompted.

After selecting your network, you'll be prompted to enter your network's password. Type it in and then click Connect. Shortly afterward, you should see the network panel icon change to a Wi-Fi signal strength icon. A message should pop-up in the top-right corner of the desktop stating that the connection was successfully established. You should test the connection by going online with the Chromium browser. The default homepage is the Google search engine, so you should see that day's Google doodle, if applicable, and be able to perform a search.

Updating TinkerOS

Now that you're online, it's good practice to check for any updates for TinkerOS. These could include updated plug-ins, applications, or even security patches. This can be done easily thru the terminal. Navigate to System Tools and select LXTerminal.

Note   As previously stated, we'll be using the terminal quite a bit going forward, so you may want to add it as a panel at the bottom of the desktop by using the Add/Remove Panel Items feature discussed earlier in this chapter.

Once you have a new terminal window open, type `sudo apt-get update` and hit Enter. This updates the list of packages available for installation. You'll see a progress percentage as a list of programs populates in the terminal window. When it's finished it will say that it's done, and you'll have your text prompt available again as shown in Figure 4-12.

Figure 4-12. *Your terminal window should look similar to this as your first updates finish downloading. Notice that it says "Done" when it's finished.*

The next command we'll use is sudo apt-get upgrade. This begins the installation process for the updates that were fetched by the previous command, sudo apt-get update.

After that process finishes, enter sudo reboot to reboot the system and ensure that everything has installed properly. This should bring you quickly back into the desktop environment with everything up to date.

Video Playback

One of the great things about TinkerOS and the Tinker Board's hardware is their ability to function as a low-powered desktop computer in a tiny package. Let's start exploring some of this functionality, first with video playback.

YouTube

To start our video test, navigate to Chromium and go to YouTube to select a video to watch. When your video starts playing, try to change the quality to 1080p. Even with a reliable Internet connection, you'll more than likely notice that the video is very choppy. If you look at the CPU usage in the bottom panel, you'll also notice that it's maxed at 100%. If you lower the video to 720p, you'll also experience less than smooth playback.

Why is this happening on a board that advertises 4K/30FPS playback? Well, it needs a driver to be installed for video rendering that will be recognized by Chromium and other programs so that the GPU can take on some of the load from the CPU. The driver we'll be using is the Mesa 3D graphics library, which will be installed via the terminal. The Mesa library is open source and, in this case, we're going to be installing the OpenGL branch of the library, which will work well with the Mali-T760 GPU on the Tinker Board.

Mesa Driver Installation

This installation process for the Mesa Driver Package is very simple. First, open a new terminal window and enter

```
sudo apt-get install libgl1-mesa-dev
```

Let the installation process run its course and then, since the Mesa driver is an important change for TinkerOS, we're going to check for any dependency updates, install those updates, and then reboot.

This is a good practice to follow any time you install a new program or driver package that marks a major change for your OS. To do this, we'll use the three terminal commands that we've used already to update the system: `sudo apt-get update`, `sudo apt-get upgrade`, and `sudo reboot`.

After rebooting, try going back to YouTube to watch the same video you just tried. You should be able to watch in perfect 1080p now. You'll also notice that the CPU usage monitor panel is no longer displaying a bottlenecked CPU. Instead, it should be hovering around 50%, a huge difference.

If for some reason your video of choice is still having problems but other videos are playing properly, you may need to install a Chromium extension that forces YouTube to play videos back in the H.264 video codec, which is ideal for Mesa drivers. This should be installed and enabled by default; however, for troubleshooting purposes it's good to keep in mind.

You can check your current codec playback format by right-clicking your video and selecting "stats for nerds" to see the display shown in Figure 4-13. It should show the avc1 format, which means it is playing back in the H.264 codec. If it isn't in H.264 or you want to be sure that videos always play in that codec in the future, you can install the h264ify extension.

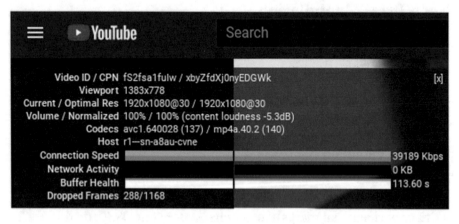

Figure 4-13. *The "stats for nerds" view on YouTube*

The simplest way to install the extension is from the Chrome store in the browser. Perform a Google search for "h264ify" and click on the link to the Chrome Web Store. Once you're at h264ify's page in the store, click on + Add to Chrome in the upper-right corner, as shown in Figure 4-14, and then agree to add the extension in the next pop-up window. After this, your YouTube playback problems should be solved.

Figure 4-14. *The Google Play download page for h264ify*

Note   The resolution at which you can play back video will also be determined by your monitor or TV's resolution capabilities.

VLC Media Player

Of course, you can also play your own video files on the Tinker Board. Simply load your video files onto a USB storage device and you'll be able to access and play them. There is a built-in media player that is pre-installed on TinkerOS, with the self-explanatory title of Media Player. It works well, but we're going to install a third-party media player to supplement it and use, called VLC.

VLC (Video LAN Codec) is an open source media player that you may have used on Windows or macOS as well. It has support for a wide variety of video codecs and has a lot of specialized features. It is also one of the standard media players used for Linux operating systems.

We're going to install VLC from the terminal using the command

```
sudo apt-get install vlc browser-plugin-vlc
```

following the current directions from VLC's web site. You may have noticed that we've entered two programs to install at once, the VLC player and a VLC browser plug-in. If you're new to Linux, this is allowed; when installing multiple programs, you just need to leave a space in between each program. Of course, the more programs you list, the greater chance there is of a typo, so be sure to check your command before hitting Enter.

After the installation has completed, we will again run `sudo apt-get update`, `sudo apt-get upgrade`, and `sudo reboot`, because VLC also installs video codec dependencies. After rebooting, if you navigate to the Sound and Video programs on the panel, you'll see that VLC was automatically added to the list as shown in Figure 4-15. From here, you can launch VLC and try playing some video files with it.

Figure 4-15. *The VLC media player has been automatically added to the Sound & Video category*

Audio

You may have just tested audio while playing videos on YouTube or with your own video files in VLC. But in case you didn't, or you had issues with audio coming thru, let's make sure that your audio preferences are set up correctly and then look at the built-in music player LXMusic.

First, choose how you're going to listen to audio. The most popular options are the 3.5mm audio jack or thru HDMI if you're using a TV or a monitor with built-in speakers as a display. Navigate to the Sound and Video panel again and select Pulse Audio Volume Control. Despite the name, this control is much more powerful than simply adjusting volume. It's here that you can select audio inputs and outputs and control settings for each device.

On the Playback tab, you'll see all the programs that are open and have the capability to transmit sound, as shown in Figure 4-16. For each program, there is a box you can click to list the available audio devices. The naming conventions for each device are not always obvious; for example, "Headset" is the 3.5mm audio jack and "Rockchip.miniarm-codec analog stereo" is the HDMI audio.

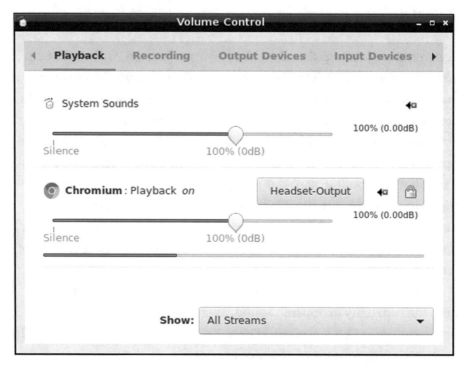

Figure 4-16. *The Playback tab in the Volume Control utility is where you can see which playback device is active and its volume level*

Once you've selected your device, you can go to the Input Devices tab to control volume. What's nice about the Pulse Audio Volume Control utility is that the 100% setting is equivalent to 0 dB, which from an audio technology perspective is quite helpful in making sure that your audio levels will be optimized for media playback. Most professionally produced audio is normalized to 0 dB, so you will be hearing sound at its intended volume if left at 100%.

Now that your device has been selected, let's launch LXMusic, which is in the Sound and Video category panel. Keep the Pulse Audio Volume Control utility opened to make sure that your preferred playback device has been selected for LXMusic, which shows up as XMMS2. After LXMusic opens, you'll see that there is one creative-commons licensed song included, by the artist Silence, as shown in Figure 4-17. Click the Play button at the top of the window, and you should hear the song coming through your selected output.

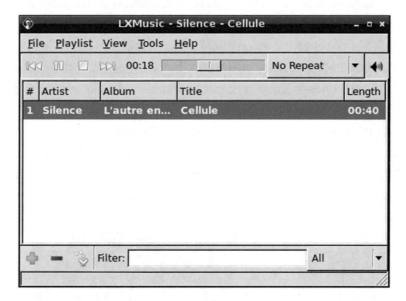

Figure 4-17. *The LXMusic interface with the included song "Cellule" by Silence*

As you can with your video files, you can also load your personal audio files onto the Tinker Board via USB and play them thru LXMusic. VLC also has audio-only support, but the GUI for LXMusic shares a lot of qualities and features with traditional desktop music players that are also found on Windows and macOS.

LibreOffice

With the availability of video and audio playback, you can start to see that the Tinker Board could be used as a desktop computer replacement for low-powered tasks. But what if you want to get some work done? Of course, we can't install Microsoft software, such as Word, or Apple software, such as Keynote. But we can install the open source Linux equivalent: LibreOffice.

LibreOffice is a suite of office productivity software that is open source and available on Linux operating systems. It's also incredibly easy to install. Simply open a new terminal window and enter sudo apt-get install libreoffice. After the installation finishes, enter the commands sudo apt-get update, sudo apt-get upgrade and sudo reboot to ensure a successful and complete installation.

After rebooting, open the menu panel and you'll see that a new category called 'Office' has been added to the listing. Just like when we installed VLC, all the LibreOffice programs have been automatically added as shortcut panels, as shown in Figure 4-18.

Figure 4-18. *The new Office category with all of the LibreOffice programs*

A Quick Tour

There are six programs in the LibreOffice suite. Going down the list that appears in the Office menu panel, the first program is LibreOffice Base, which allows you to create searchable databases. Next is LibreOffice Calc, which is a spreadsheet program like Microsoft Excel, followed by LibreOffice Draw, which allows you to create diagrams, as shown in Figure 4-19.

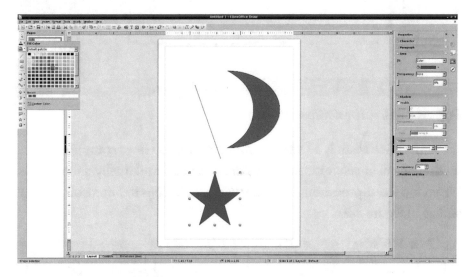

Figure 4-19. *LibreOffice Draw*

After that is LibreOffice Impress, which lets you create slideshows, as you would with Microsoft PowerPoint or Apple Keynote; it is shown in Figure 4-20.

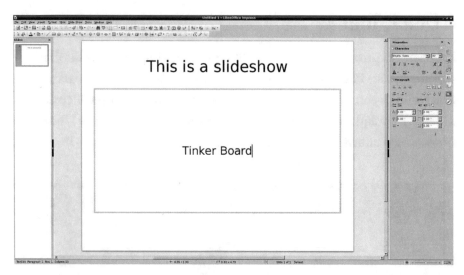

Figure 4-20. *LibreOffice Impress*

LibreOffice Math is a formula editor, in case you have complex mathematical or scientific formulas to document. And finally, LibreOffice Writer is a word-processing program with similarities to Microsoft Word as shown in Figure 4-21.

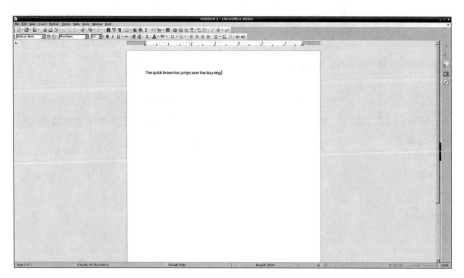

Figure 4-21. *LibreOffice Writer*

As you can probably tell, the LibreOffice suite is quite extensive and doesn't hold back in features. These aren't "bad actor" pieces of software; you can get real work done with them.[1] With this suite of software installed, we're on our way to having a fully decked out tiny Linux computer.

Fun and Games

To act as a desktop replacement, though, we need to make sure that you can have fun and relax with TinkerOS. After all, what is a computer without games; especially classics like Solitaire and Minesweeper? We're going to install a gaming suite called Ace of Penguins, which has open source versions of classic old school stock computer games, such as Penguin Freecell and the previously mentioned Solitaire and Minesweeper; now referred to as Penguin Solitaire and Penguin Minesweeper. All the games feature a penguin mascot, a nod to the Linux mascot Tux.

Note   If you don't want to have any games installed on TinkerOS because you see the Tinker Board as serious business or you're afraid of the temptation, don't worry. This installation isn't integral to following any of the upcoming tutorials; it's just a little Easter egg.

It would be a shame if installing something fun was difficult; and luckily, like the other installations we've looked at so far, Ace of Penguins is also very simple. As usual, open a new terminal window and then enter `sudo apt-get install ace-of-penguins`. Note the dashes in the program name. After the installation runs its course you can do the usual `sudo apt-get update`, `sudo apt-get upgrade` and `sudo reboot`, but it isn't entirely necessary for this package.

---

[1]There is a lot more information about LibreOffice available on their web site: `libreoffice.org`

To find your newly installed games, navigate to the menu panel and you'll see that there has been another category automatically added; it's appropriately titled Games, as shown in Figure 4-22.

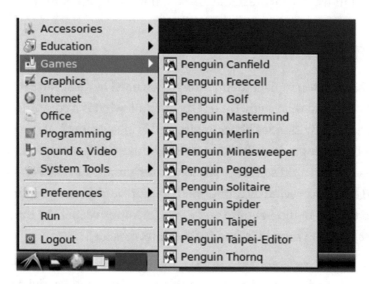

Figure 4-22. *The new Games category*

As you can see, the library is quite extensive, and if you were a Windows or Apple computer user in the 1990s, then many of these will be familiar to you. The games are responsive and look a lot like the classics. For example, Penguin Solitaire, as shown in Figure 4-23, features the familiar drag and drop action for the cards.

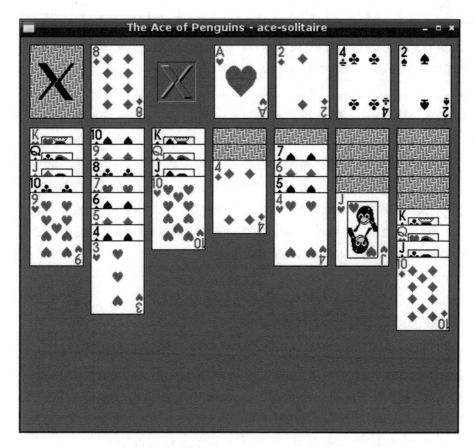

Figure 4-23. *Penguin Solitaire*

Hello World, Let's Get Back to Work

They say to keep a healthy mind it's important to incorporate play and breaks into your routine, so after a quick game of Penguin Solitaire you should feel refreshed and ready to tackle our final task for this chapter: programming!

The Tinker Board can support any programming language for development, just like any other Linux computer; however, we're going to focus mainly on Python and a little bit on C. These languages will be especially useful with the Tinker Board because there are libraries for both C and Python to use and interact with the GPIO pins, which we'll be experimenting with in the next chapter.

Note   This book does not include a coding tutorial for either language. It is assumed that you have some basic coding experience and can recognize things like functions, arrays, if statements, and so on. If you are new to coding, though, don't worry. There are many open source resources available to help you with coding in either C or Python, and the code used for projects in this book will not be too advanced for a beginner to understand.

Installing an IDE for C

There are some preinstalled IDEs for coding in TinkerOS, but there isn't one for C. For our purposes we're going to install Geany. There are many different IDEs to choose from, and everyone is going to have different preferences; so if there is an IDE that you prefer, feel free to install and use it. Geany is a fairly basic IDE and will be great for beginners.

The installation is simple. Again, open a new terminal window and this time enter sudo apt-get install geany. After the installation finishes, navigate to the menu panel and click Programming. You'll see that Geany has automatically populated as a shortcut, as shown in Figure 4-24.

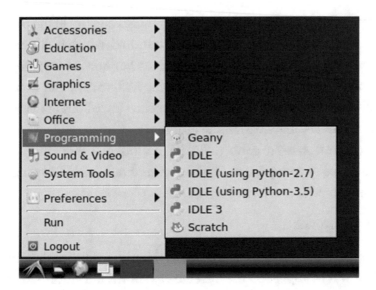

Figure 4-24. *As you can see, Geany has been added to the Programming category*

Open Geany and you'll see that it has all the features you'd expect a standard IDE to have. Feel free to explore to get a feel for it if you aren't familiar with IDEs. We're going to use it to run some example code with the GPIO pins in the next chapter.

Python Test

Although we had to install an IDE in order to use C, we don't have to do that for Python, because multiple instances of IDLE, a Python-specific IDE, are installed. Each version is denoted by a number, which corresponds to a generation of Python; all of which have slightly different features and conventions. There are strong preferences among the Python community for the different versions, but for our purposes we'll use the newest version, Python 3. If you are an experienced Python user and prefer an earlier version you can certainly use it, but you may need to adjust certain lines of code going forward.

To open IDLE, navigate to the Programming category in the menu panel to select it. This will open a Python terminal, which is different from the IDE where we'll be writing programs later. For now, we're going to test the terminal. It has a lot in common with the LXTerminal that we've used to install programs in that it allows you to send single lines of Python code and get instant feedback within the terminal.

To run our test, we're going to do the traditional first coding experience: we're going to have Python write "hello world". To do this, we're going to print a string; which in Python syntax is

```
print ("hello world")
```

After you type that into the Python terminal, hit Enter and you should see hello world appear on the next line, as shown in Figure 4-25. If your terminal looks like that figure, congratulations! You've just written a line of Python code on the Tinker Board!

Figure 4-25. *Hello world in the Python IDLE terminal*

Later we'll write more advanced programs, and in the next chapter
we'll experiment with simple GPIO controls with Python and C scripts.
This is where the fun begins, and you'll get to experience the true potential
of the Tinker Board as a fully programmable tool for projects.

Conclusion

After a lot of preparation, we've finally started using the Tinker Board. By now you should be feeling at least a little bit comfortable navigating around TinkerOS. There are, of course, countless other programs you can install and use to have the Tinker Board act as a desktop computer. As we go forward we'll be concentrating more on projects, which will involve coding and the GPIO pins, which we'll be discussing next.

These exercises and projects will be more involved and technical tasks. As a result, they will probably be more fun and exciting for you than many of the items we discussed in this chapter. However, to think that a board of this size can run a full desktop operating system with all of these features and functionality is quite the technological feat when you think about it. I hope seeing it in action has spurred your curiosity, and you're ready to see what else it can do.

CHAPTER 5

Programming with the GPIO Pins

Now that we've gotten a feel for TinkerOS, we can look a little deeper at the functionality of the Tinker Board, specifically with programming and the GPIO pins. We discussed what the GPIO pins are in Chapter 1, but to refresh, the GPIO (general purpose input and output) pins are the exposed pins along the edge of the Tinker Board. All of them are numbered and have different functionality, which is expressed by a color directly under the pin. For example, 5V pins have a red pad underneath them and ground pins have a black pad, as shown in Figure 5-1.

Figure 5-1. *The Tinker Board's GPIO pins. Notice the color coding on the header to easily identify each pin's function.*

© Liz Clark 2019
L. Clark, *Practical Tinker Board*, https://doi.org/10.1007/978-1-4842-3826-4_5

The GPIO pins can be controlled by programs that you can write in either C or Python, the two programming languages we've briefly discussed in the preceding chapter. ASUS has libraries available for each language to communicate easily between your program and the GPIO pins. We'll be installing these shortly via the terminal. To fully utilize the GPIO pins, though, you'll need some basic hobby electronics components. You may already have these if you've worked on electronics projects before, but let's go through them to be on the safe side.

Gathering Supplies

If you've never built an electronic circuit before, this section of the chapter will serve as your crash course into the world of electronics from a practical hobby standpoint, including where to source your components, which components to buy (for the purposes of this chapter), and any other odds and ends you may find to be useful when experimenting with controlling circuits with the Tinker Board. If you're an experienced electronics tinkerer, you can more than likely sit back and relax during this portion and jump back in when we get to setting up the code libraries in TinkerOS.

Your first question when thinking about electronic components for the first time is probably going to be where you buy this stuff. As brick-and-mortar hobby stores continue to become a rarity, it can be hard to run out and buy these items. Luckily, there are many companies to choose from online to purchase from. Some popular ones include Adafruit, Sparkfun, Mouser, Digikey, and of course Amazon and similar large online retailers such as eBay. Adafruit and Sparkfun offer a more maker-friendly selection of components and other electronic delights, whereas Mouser and Digikey tend to cater to the more professional electronics enthusiasts and engineers; however it can be helpful to keep them in mind when you can't find a specific part. Amazon offers a wide selection from many different resellers varying in size. Depending on the seller, quality can be varied;

so always research and shop smart, especially when it comes to electronics. You don't want to buy questionable parts because the price was right, only to waste hours troubleshooting temperamental or nonfunctional equipment and parts.

Now that you know where to buy, *what* do you need to buy? Let's go over some basic yet necessary parts that will get you started.

LEDs

One of the most versatile and fun electronic components of all time is the humble LED (light-emitting diode). Coming in a variety of shapes and sizes, LEDs can serve a plethora of purposes in a circuit, often serving as a simple indicator or being the main attraction in a large-scale LED matrix display. We'll be using LEDs more as indicators here, and in fact they'll play a starring role in our first circuit that we build with the Tinker Board.

Resistors

Another common component is a resistor. Resistors limit the electrical current passing through a circuit. They're important to protect more fragile components, like LEDs, from receiving too much voltage. Resistors can have different values, which are expressed in ohms and denoted by the different colored bands on the body of the resistor. The value that we'll use for these circuits is 220Ω, which has two red bands followed by a brown band, as shown later in the circuit diagrams for the examples.

Photoresistor

A photoresistor is a type of resistor whose resistance is determined by the amount of light hitting the sensor. By exposing it to increased or decreased light, you can produce different results in a circuit.

Buttons and Switches

We'll use buttons to control different aspects of the circuit with code. There are two types of buttons: temporary and latching. A temporary button only affects a circuit while held down, while a latching switch remains engaged and must be pressed again to return to its previous state, like a light switch. The type of button that you use is up to you, but in the circuit pictures in this chapter you'll see breadboard-friendly temporary buttons and latching switches to easily denote the difference visually.

Capacitors

Finally, another common component is the capacitor. A capacitor, sometimes called a cap, stores potential energy, which is referred to as capacitance. Capacitance can then be added back into a circuit. The cap itself has two leads, which may or may not be polarized depending on the type.

Connecting Your Circuits to the Tinker Board

There are, of course, many more electrical components available than the short list that we mentioned. But with these basic components, we'll be able to get started programming the Tinker Board and using the GPIO pins to see what the code is doing in real time.

How, then, do we build a circuit and connect it to the Tinker Board for control? First, we'll need to build the circuit on what's referred to as a *solderless breadboard,* or *breadboard* for short. Breadboards are used for electronic prototyping. They're plastic trays with evenly spaced holes that are sized to fit through-hole components with 0.1" (2.54mm) pitch, meaning that they have metal leads spaced to fit the pitches of holes on both PCBs and breadboards with that spacing. These holes in the breadboard allow components to contact metal rails that are embedded in the plastic housing, usually in rows, to carry current to each component to have a stable circuit. Breadboards can be found at the same suppliers referenced earlier for electronic components and come in a variety of shapes, sizes, layouts, and even colors.

Chances are that when you lay your components out on a breadboard, they won't be able to comfortably reach each other to make contact. This is where jumper wires come in. Jumper wires allow you to make the electrical connections between components and the Tinker Board, which in this scenario will be transmitting data, power and ground connections to the breadboard. Jumper wires are specially made to be reused in prototyping situations, since they are of pre-cut lengths and have plastic headers on either end.

There are three types of jumper wire: male-to-male, male-to-female, and female-to-female. Male-to-male is probably the most common, since it's basically just a piece of wire and can be used to make connections across the breadboard. Male-to-female and female-to-female can extend connections between components that have headers or components that are farther away from each other. We'll use female-to-male wires to connect the GPIO header from the Tinker Board to the breadboard.

Note   There are GPIO extension cables sold for the Raspberry Pi family of boards that you could use with the Tinker Board since they have the same GPIO pinout. These allow you to use a ribbon cable that has a large female header on one end that fits over all the GPIO pins and male headers at the other end to plug directly into the breadboard. In this chapter, however, it will be assumed that you're just using female-to-male jumper wire to interface your circuits with the GPIO pins.

Circuit Diagrams

The examples throughout this book will include circuit diagrams so that you can build the circuits accurately. These diagrams were all created with Fritzing, an open source program that allows you to create circuit diagrams to display a circuit in breadboard, schematic, or printed-circuit board (PCB) view. For the upcoming examples we will use the breadboard view, since it allows the circuit to be easily expressed as a picture with the components.

Besides including images for standard components, Fritzing also allows the creation of custom parts that can be used in your circuits and diagrams. A custom Tinker Board part has been created for this book and will be available for download so that you can add it to your Fritzing part library, if you wish, for your future projects with the Tinker Board.

Installing Programming Libraries in TinkerOS

Let's take a break from hardware for a moment and go back to software. Before we can start coding, we need to install some libraries for the coding languages that can interface with the GPIO pins, Python and C. To do this, we're going to boot into TinkerOS and open a terminal window to install the libraries using the git clone command to download and clone the repositories from GitHub to your local OS. These libraries will make programming for the GPIO pins very simple, similar to using an Arduino or Raspberry Pi. In fact, the libraries are heavily based or even direct ports of the libraries available for Raspberry Pi.

Installing the Python Library

First we're going to install the Python library. Python is a general-purpose programming language whose syntax is set up to be easy to read, so users can understand what's happening in the code at a glance. Because of this, it's a great text-based programming language to get started with.

Navigate to your terminal window and enter in our favorite commands from the previous chapter: `sudo apt-get update` and `sudo apt-get upgrade`. This ensures that everything is up to date, so that when we install our Python library it is set up in the best possible scenario.

After any updates you fetch have finished installing, we're going to install the Python language packages, which contain dependencies needed to properly code in Python using IDLE, the Python IDE, and the ability to use any extensions within Python. We'll install the packages for both Python 2.7 and Python 3. To install, enter `sudo apt-get install python-dev python2.7-dev python3-dev` into the terminal. You'll notice that we're installing both at the same time.

After the Python packages have been installed, we're going to install Git, open source software that allows you to keep track of multiple files in a project so that they can be edited in real time by multiple users on different computers. Git has become an industry standard for code project management. As mentioned previously, these libraries will be cloned from their repositories on GitHub, a popular website used to host projects using Git. To install Git, enter `sudo apt-get install git` into the terminal.

Note   Entire books have been written on how to use Git to its full potential along with the associated websites, such as GitHub. Here we'll only be discussing the basic uses that will be necessary for our use case in accessing these code libraries.

Now that all the dependencies have been installed, we can finally get to installing the Python library. In the terminal, enter

```
git clone https://github.com/TinkerBoard/gpio_lib_python.git
```

You'll see the installation begin, and after a few moments the Python library will be downloaded to your installation of TinkerOS.

If you navigate to the file directory GUI, you'll see the folder that we just cloned, as shown in Figure 5-2. However, you'll also see that the folder is zipped and needs to be unzipped to be usable. Going back to the terminal, enter unzip python. Now you'll see that a new unzipped folder has appeared in the file directory called gpio_lib_python.

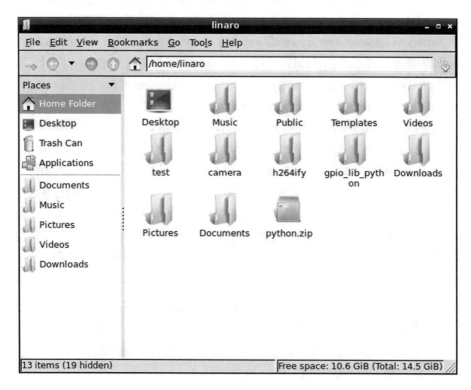

Figure 5-2. *The Python code library folders, both zipped and unzipped, in the Home folder directory*

There is just one more step before the Python library is ready to use. We need to run the included setup script in the folder to sync the library with the Python language libraries that we installed a few steps back. To do this, we'll use the terminal to change directories to the unzipped folder; enter

```
cd /home/linaro/gpio_lib_python
```

You'll notice that the terminal now shows that you are working inside that folder instead of the default file directory, as shown in Figure 5-3. Now that we're in the folder we're going to run the setup.py script, which you can see in the file directory GUI by entering sudo python setup.py install.

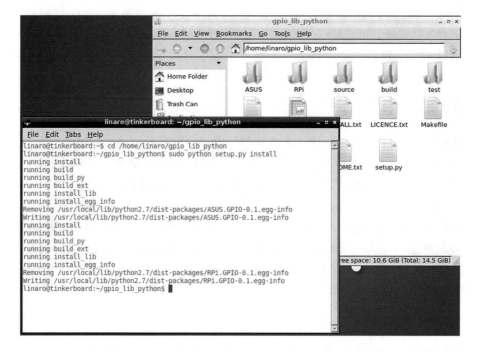

Figure 5-3. *The terminal after changing directories to the new gpio_ lib_python folder and running the* sudo python setup.py install *command*

After that finishes running, we're going to run the script for Python 2.7 and Python 3, by entering sudo `python2.7 setup.py install` followed by sudo `python3 setup.py install`.

Blink!

We're finally ready to build some circuits and write some code. The first example we're going to look at is commonly referred to as Blink and is considered the hardware version of "Hello World!" It's a very simple program that will make an LED blink by regularly causing the GPIO's data pin, which the LED will be connected to, to go high and low (or on and off) repeatedly. It's a great test to make sure that everything is set up correctly on the Tinker Board for software and to also make sure that your hardware is configured properly as well.

Build the Circuit

Since this is the first circuit we're building we're going to prep the breadboard and other components that we'll use repeatedly as we learn about the GPIO pins. Take your breadboard and two male-to-female jumper wires. Plug the first male end into the ground rail and the second male end into the power rail on the breadboard. Then take the female ends and plug them into the corresponding GPIO pins; ground to ground and power to 5V, as shown in Figure 5-4. To make things easier visually, ground GPIO pins are marked as black and 5V pins are marked as red.

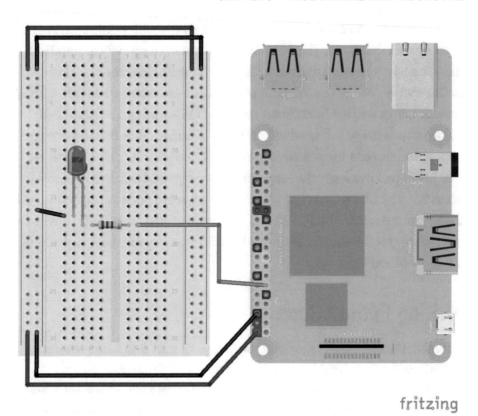

fritzing

Figure 5-4. *The circuit diagram used to blink an LED. Notice how the 5V and ground rails are set up, as well as the LED's polarity and connection to physical GPIO pin 11 on the Tinker Board.*

Note   Going forward it will be assumed that you have your breadboard wired up like this to power and ground unless otherwise noted.

Now we can take the LED and place it on the breadboard so that each leg is on a different rail. The LED can't be connected directly to the GPIO pins, though; it needs a resistor to limit the current that can pass through it. Otherwise, the LED could short out and die. As discussed earlier, a 220Ω resistor works well for breadboarding basic LEDs and can be identified by two bands of red followed by one band of brown. Take this resistor and connect it between the positive leg of the LED and GPIO physical pin 11. The LED's positive leg is the longer of its two legs and is called an anode. Then take the LED's other leg, which has a negative polarity, and connect it to the ground rail on the breadboard. A negative lead on an LED is called a cathode and is the shorter of its two legs. After you're finished, your circuit should look like Figure 5-4.

Writing Python Code

Now that the electronics are wired properly, let's get into some coding in Python. Navigate to the Programs menu under Programming and open IDLE (using Python-2.7). As mentioned previously, there are a few different versions of IDLE installed in TinkerOS; and we did install the GPIO Python library for both Python 2.7 and 3, but at the time of writing all the code examples that we're about to go through have been tested to work with Python 2.7.

When you first open IDLE, a shell window will open, which we looked at briefly at the end of Chapter 4. This is the terminal for writing lines of Python code in real time and for debugging purposes. We'll need to open a new file to write a program that we'll be able to run. To do this, click File and then New File in the upper-left corner of the shell window. This opens a new IDE window with Untitled at the top. Let's save this file as "blink" in the "test" folder that lives inside the gpio_lib_python folder that we've been working with. Other pieces of Python example code are saved in there as well, as shown in Figure 5-5.

Figure 5-5. *Saving what will become our new Python program to the test folder within the Python GPIO library folder. Notice that we are naming it "blink."*

Now we have a saved blank Python file staring back at us. This can be a bit intimidating for first-time programmers, but if we take it step by step we should be blinking the LED in no time. First, we need to import the code libraries that we'll be referencing in our program. We'll of course be using the GPIO library that we just installed, as well as the built-in time library for Python that allows us to insert delays, which will be essential for blinking our LED. To do this in Python, we're going to enter the following:

```
import ASUS.GPIO as GPIO
import time
```

The next line in the program is a bit of a workaround that you may choose to leave out from future programs as you gain more experience:

```
GPIO.setwarnings(False)
```

This turns off warnings about any issues with any of the GPIO pins before the program runs. If a program is exited in an incorrect way (think of turning off a desktop computer by holding down the power button while running multiple applications), then the GPIO pins (or ports when discussing them in terms of the SoC) can become "stuck" and appear to be in use by your system, in this case by TinkerOS. By including that line of code at the beginning of your program you can ignore those errors and avoid frustrations while getting started. Keep in mind, though, that this does not fix the problem and in a best-case scenario you should be ending your programs properly and always fully debugging for long-term program use.

Now we need to tell the board which numbering sequence we'll use for identifying the GPIO pins. There are two modes that can be set: `GPIO.BOARD` and `GPIO.ASUS`. `GPIO.BOARD` uses the physical GPIO pin's numbers to identify them in the code. So if you were to connect a component to pin 3, then you would be able to call pin 3 in your code. The `GPIO.ASUS` numbering sequence is in reference to the SoC's numbering channels for each GPIO pin. These numbers do not match the physical numbers, and the result can be confusing. For example, physical pin 3 is called pin 252 when using `GPIO.ASUS`. For the purposes of our exercises here, we'll use the `GPIO.BOARD` method, since it's more intuitive. To set this up in the program, type on a new line

```
GPIO.setmode(GPIO.BOARD)
```

Note If you've programmed the GPIO pins on a Raspberry Pi before, this will be familiar to you since for the Pi there are also two modes: BOARD and BCM, where BCM is the equivalent to GPIO.ASUS. You can bring up a detailed diagram of the GPIO.BOARD and GPIO.ASUS numbers by entering `sudo gpio readall` in the terminal, as you'll see in Figure 5-15, after installing the C library, which we will also go through later in the chapter.

With the numbering mode selected, we're going to set up the LED's GPIO pin with two lines of code. First, we'll define which pin the LED is connected to, by entering:

```
LED = 11
```

With the pin defined, we now need to set up the pin to be an output, since we're going to send a signal through it rather than receive a signal as we would with a button or other similar component. To do this we'll use this line of code:

```
GPIO.setup(LED, GPIO.OUT)
```

Because we've told our program previously that we're going to refer to pin 11 as LED, we can use it as a placeholder whenever we refer to the pin in our program. At this point we have coded in all of our dependencies, and your code should look something like this, as also shown in Figure 5-6.

Figure 5-6. *Our blink.py script so far*

```
import ASUS.GPIO as GPIO
import time

GPIO.setwarnings(False)

GPIO.setmode(GPIO.BOARD)

LED = 11

GPIO.setup(LED, GPIO.OUT)
```

Now it's time to code in the blinking portion of the code, more commonly known as the loop. We're going to set up our loop to run infinitely, one of the few times that this will be a goal, so that the LED will in theory blink forever by alternating the status of the LED's GPIO pin from high (3.3V) to low (0V) or on and off. To accomplish this, we're going to put all our blink code inside a while True: statement. For debugging purposes we're also going to print in the terminal whether the LED is supposed to be on or off to make sure our circuit is behaving as expected. This is good practice for debugging any code, especially as you move on to more complicated projects. This loop will look like this:

```
while True:
        GPIO.output(LED, GPIO.HIGH)
        print("led on")
        time.sleep(1)
        GPIO.output(LED, GPIO.LOW)
        print("led off")
        time.sleep(1)
```

Here is the first time we're using the Time library, by adding a delay of one second, so that the LED will be on and off for one second each continually. The print statement allows us to send whatever text is between the quotation marks to the terminal as text. This loop will work on its own, but it will make for better code if we add two more lines.

If you remember back to the beginning of this program, we added the GPIO.setwarnings(False) line in case any of the GPIO pins get stuck in the event of a program being improperly shut down. We're going to add some lines now to try to ensure that a proper shutdown can occur for this program, especially since it is set up to run infinitely. We're going to use try: ... except to encase the loop, with the exception being that in the event of a keyboard interrupt the script will end and the GPIO pins will reset to their default states. For Python, the key combination of Control + C can stop the script via the terminal and by including the keyboard interrupt it will simultaneously trigger the GPIO pins to reset. Now with these parameters our loop will look like this:

```
try:
    while True:
            GPIO.output(LED, GPIO.HIGH)
            print("led on")
            time.sleep(1)
            GPIO.output(LED, GPIO.LOW)
            print("led off")
            time.sleep(1)
except KeyboardInterrupt: GPIO.cleanup()
```

Your full code should now look like this:

```
import ASUS.GPIO as GPIO
import time

GPIO.setwarnings(False)

GPIO.setmode(GPIO.BOARD)

LED = 11

GPIO.setup(LED, GPIO.OUT)

try:
    while True:
            GPIO.output(LED, GPIO.HIGH)
            print("led on")
            time.sleep(1)
            GPIO.output(LED, GPIO.LOW)
            print("led off")
            time.sleep(1)
except KeyboardInterrupt: GPIO.cleanup()
```

Congratulations! You've written your first Python program on the Tinker Board! Now save your script and let's move over to the terminal to run it.

Running Your Code

In the terminal, change your target directory to the test folder where you've saved your Blink program, by entering cd /home/linaro/gpio_lib_python/test. There are two ways to run Python scripts from the terminal. The first requires you to add this line at the top of your program:

```
#!/usr/bin/env python
```

So that the beginning of your program would look like this:

```
#!/usr/bin/env python

import ASUS.GPIO as GPIO
import time
```

If you're using this method, add that line to the top of your program and save it. Then, in the terminal, enter chmod +x blink.py once to change the execution mode to that of Python program so that it can be run as an executable with sudo ./blink.py. If you do not want to add that line to your program, you can run Python scripts with the line sudo python blink.py. After choosing your method, enter it into the terminal; you should see your LED begin to blink, and the terminal should display alternating lines of "led on" and "led off" as shown in Figure 5-7.

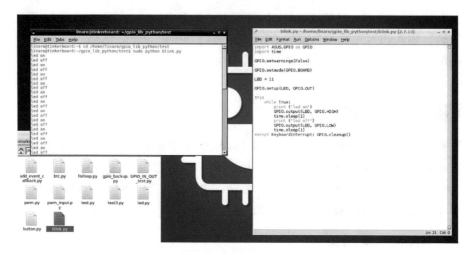

Figure 5-7. *The blink.py program running*

Add a Button

Blinking an LED is great, but chances are your projects will require more than a flashing light. We can modify both the Blink program and circuit slightly to have a button control when the LED is on rather than software.

To do this, we'll first add in a button to our breadboard. Any temporary state button will do, whether it be a traditional breadboard spaced button or a giant clicky arcade button. Plug one of the button's leads into the ground rail on the breadboard and the other lead to GPIO pin 13; right next to the LED as shown in Figure 5-8.

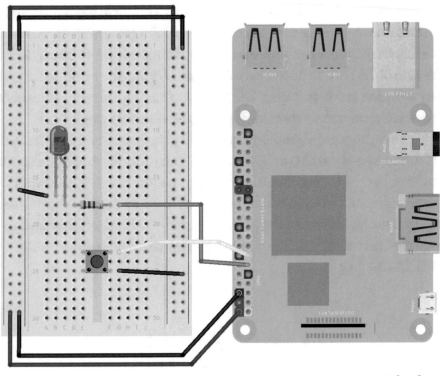

fritzing

Figure 5-8. *The LED circuit with a button added. Notice that the button is connected to both ground and GPIO physical pin 13 next to the LED*

To program the button, we're going to edit the Blink program we just wrote since we're still using the LED. We're going to define the button as GPIO pin 13 and an input by adding the lines:

```
button = 13
```

```
GPIO.setup(button.GPIO.IN)
```

We still want the loop to run infinitely since we want to be able to press the button at any time to turn on the LED. But we're going to check to see whether the button is being pressed and have the state of the button affect the state of the LED. To do this we will use an if/else statement, which is very common in programming. The logic is defined by having two situations to check for; commonly checking for things like sensors being on or off.

For our program, we're going to say that if the button is read as false, or off, then we want the LED to be turned on. This probably sounds incorrect; however, because of the circuit we're using and how the GPIO pins work, the default state of the pin is true or on, and as a result we need to tell the logic to look for the button to be "off" to turn the LED on. We also need to have the LED be off when the button is not pressed. Our loop as a result will look like this:

```
try:
    while True:
        if GPIO.input(button) == False:
            GPIO.output(LED, True)
            print("pressed")
            time.sleep(.1)
        else:
            GPIO.output(LED, False)
            print("off")
            time.sleep(.1)
except KeyboardInterrupt: GPIO.cleanup()
```

You'll see that the delay has been reduced to 0.1 second. This makes the response time a lot faster, since if it were to be kept at 1 second there would be a significant delay between when you pressed the button and when the LED finally lit up, and vice-versa. We've also added in two terminal print-outs to double check the state of the code compared to your circuit. However, with the decreased delay, please keep in mind that these print-outs will move much more quickly up your terminal.

> **Note**   Notice the indents and colons in the loop. These are integral characteristics of the syntax of the Python language. Using them makes writing code in Python very simple; however, they are quite subtle and can often be missed, especially by a beginner. If you're having issues with any of your code, be sure to check your indents and colon usage first to avoid long bouts of frustrating debugging.

With this updated loop and setup, your final Button code should look like this:

```python
import ASUS.GPIO as GPIO
import time

GPIO.setwarnings(False)

GPIO.setmode(GPIO.BOARD)

LED = 11
button = 13

GPIO.setup(LED, GPIO.OUT)
GPIO.setup(button.GPIO.IN)

try:
    while True:
        if GPIO.input(button) == False:
            GPIO.output(LED, True)
            print("pressed")
            time.sleep(.1)
        else:
            GPIO.output(LED, False)
            print("off")
            time.sleep(.1)
except KeyboardInterrupt: GPIO.cleanup()
```

Since you were more than likely editing your Blink sketch, be sure to save this new program as Button in the same test folder we've been working in. After saving it, open a terminal window and change directories to the test folder as we did before. Then use your preferred method of running a Python program from earlier and run the Button.py script. Your button should be controlling your LED, and your debug statements should be quickly scrolling down your terminal.

Switch It Up

We can use the same code with a slightly different circuit to have a different effect that could be handy for future projects. We can take out the button and swap a simple switch so that the LED can stay on while the switch is engaged and of course turn off when the switch is disengaged. Take your switch and connect two of the terminals to the ground and GPIO pin 13 wires that the button was previously connected to on the breadboard, as shown in Figure 5-9. Now run the Button.py script and try out the switch.

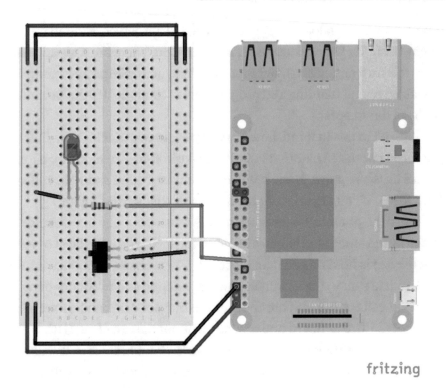

Figure 5-9. *Our button circuit now with a sliding switch*

Reading Data

There's one last example to go over and unfortunately (or fortunately) it doesn't include an LED. Instead we're going to switch gears and build a circuit around the humble photocell resistor, which we discussed a bit earlier in this chapter. We're going to use the photocell to send data to the Tinker Board that will then be displayed in the terminal. This will serve as a good example showing how to hook up other sensors in the future to the board and read data in real time.

There is a caveat in reading this data. The Tinker Board, much like other single-board computers, is incapable of reading analog signals (any signals that do not fit into the basic on or off state), because it

105

has no onboard analog to digital converter (ADC), which is found on microcontroller boards such as an Arduino Uno. There are ICs available to do this on a circuit level, but that would begin to take us into more advanced circuit building and programming realms, which are beyond the scope of this chapter.

With all of this in mind, how are we going to read analog data from a photocell resistor? This is where another basic component, a capacitor, comes in. We're going to use a 1 μF capacitor to receive and hold voltage from the GPIO pin that the photocell resistor will be attached to.

Since the photocell is basically a variable resistor whose resistance varies by the amount of light it's exposed to, it will affect the level of voltage that the cap is holding and later dispersing. This changing voltage is then read as data sent to the terminal. The cap is acting as a translator between the photocell resistor and the GPIO pin so that the data can be read in a way that the Tinker Board understands without the use of an ADC.

This isn't a solution for all analog signals, though, since as discussed, it works only because the photocell is a type of resistor. As a result, this method will only work with sensors that have similar attributes. It's also not as reliable as an ADC and can be glitchy in the data that it records, so it should only be used for applications where precise data is not a necessity. Performance will also depend on the CPU's load, with less accuracy at higher loads. Despite this, it is a great example of how you can use circuits to work around software and SoC limitations.

To build this circuit, we're going to connect one lead from the photocell to the power rail on the breadboard and the second lead to GPIO physical pin 11. We're then going to take our capacitor, which has polarity, and connect the ground leg to ground and the positive leg on the same breadboard rail as the connection to GPIO pin 11, as shown in Figure 5-10.

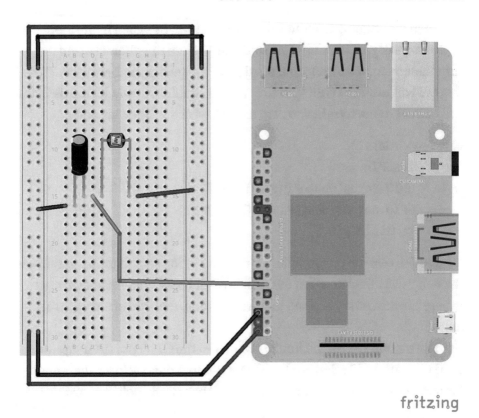

fritzing

Figure 5-10. *The photocell resistor and capacitor circuit. Notice the polarity of the capacitor, as well as the shared rail between the capacitor and the photocell.*

For the code, we're going to keep a lot of the same formatting that we've been using; including the library imports, GPIO warnings, GPIO mode and the loop setup utilizing try:, ending with the keyboard interrupt to reset the GPIO pins. But unlike our last script, we only need to define one GPIO pin. We're going to define GPIO pin 11 this way:

```
photoPin = 11
```

Then we're going to write a function that will be called in the loop to check the signal coming into GPIO pin 11 from the photocell and simultaneously store and write the data being read from that signal. To do this, we will reset the GPIO pin to zero and simultaneously set the data that will be sent to the terminal to zero as well, with the following code:

```
def sensorData():
        readPin = 0
        GPIO.setup(photoPin, GPIO.OUT)
        GPIO.output(photoPin, GPIO.LOW)
        time.sleep(0.1)
```

readPin will be our variable for the data being sent to the terminal, and the delay will affect how fast the data is read. You'll notice it's set to come in very quickly, so if you need a slower reading, feel free to increase the delay.

The second part of the function changes the GPIO pin to an input to send the data and includes a loop to record that data by inserting a math function of += 1 to affect the readPin variable. It will look like this:

```
        GPIO.setup(photoPin, GPIO.IN)

        while (GPIO.input(photoPin) == GPIO.LOW):
                readPin += 1
        return readPin
```

The return readPin command stores the data that will then be sent to the terminal in the main loop, which will be written this way:

```
try:
        while True:
                print sensorData()
except KeyboardInterrupt: GPIO.cleanup()
```

Since we did a bulk of the programming in the function, our loop can be very short; all that's left to do is make sure that the data that we're storing is being sent to the terminal. Your final program should look like this:

```
import ASUS.GPIO as GPIO
import time

GPIO.setwarnings(False)

GPIO.setmode(GPIO.BOARD)

photoPin = 11

def sensorData():
        readPin = 0
        GPIO.setup(photoPin, GPIO.OUT)
        GPIO.output(photoPin, GPIO.LOW)
        time.sleep(0.1)

        GPIO.setup(photoPin, GPIO.IN)

        while (GPIO.input(photoPin) == GPIO.LOW):
                readPin += 1
        return readPin
try:
        while True:
                print sensorData()
except KeyboardInterrupt: GPIO.cleanup()
```

Make sure to save your new program as photocell.py in the test folder that we've been using and then open a terminal window.

In the terminal, run photocell.py using your preferred method from earlier and then affect the amount of light that is hitting the photocell. When more light hits the photocell the numbers sent to the terminal will be lower and when less light is received the number is higher, as shown in Figures 5-11 and 5-12.

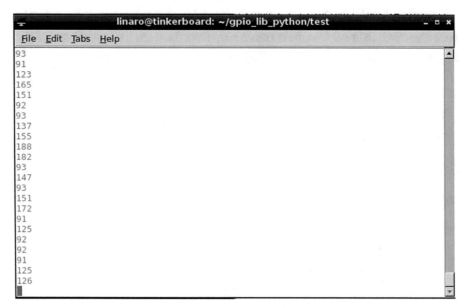

Figure 5-11. *The data sent to the terminal when the photocell resistor is exposed to a large amount of light*

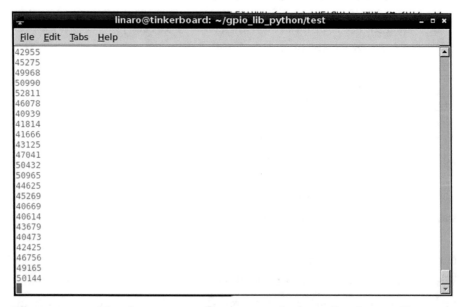

Figure 5-12. *The data sent to the terminal when the photocell resistor is exposed to little or no light*

Although they are basic in principal and composition, these circuits and corresponding programs should give you the beginning tools to form your understanding of the Tinker Board's GPIO pins and the use of the GPIO pin library for Python.

Installing the C Library

Python was fun, but there is more to explore with the GPIO pins. Next we're going to move on to the C programming language. Installing the C library for the GPIO pins is a very similar process to the Python library. Again, we're going to install the libraries via Git. Open a terminal and enter

```
git clone https://github.com/TinkerBoard/gpio_lib_c.git
```

You'll see the library go through the download and installation process.

Unlike the Python library, the C library does not download as a zipped file. Instead, it comes as a folder that needs to be decompiled using the `build` command in the terminal, which will execute a build file within the folder we just downloaded, like the way we ran the setup.py program to finish setting up the Python library.

First, we're going to change directories to our new C library folder by entering `cd /home/linaro/gpio_lib_c` into the terminal. You should see the new file extension on the left side of the terminal after this. If you look at the file directory GUI in the folder at the same time, you'll see the build file in question. Before we can execute it, we need to make it an executable file by using the change mode command that we looked at earlier with Python. Enter `chmod a+x build` into the terminal followed by `sudo ./ build` to execute the file. After this, the C library is fully set up.

The C GPIO library is heavily dependent on a port of the wiringPi library, which was written for use with the Raspberry Pi family of boards. As a result, the included examples may even reference Pi boards rather than the Tinker Board. A benefit of this is that there are more code

111

examples available than there are for the Python GPIO library, including an example of Blink in C. Let's look at this file using the Geany IDE, which we installed in the previous chapter.

Blink in C

Open the File Manager GUI and navigate to the newly installed gpio_lib_c folder that we just downloaded via Git. Once in that folder, open the examples folder inside it. In the examples folder are many programs to run on the Tinker Board using C. We're going to first look at the blink.c example. Find that file and then right-click it to open it with Geany, as shown in Figure 5-13.

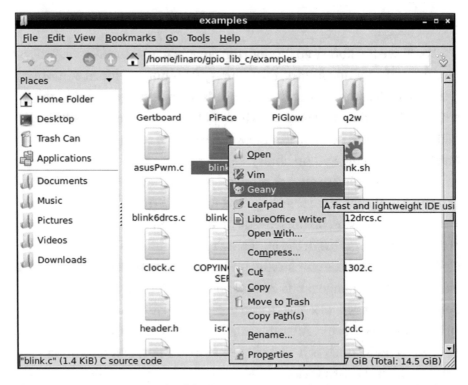

Figure 5-13. *Opening the blink.c example code that comes with the installation of the GPIO library for C. We're opening it with Geany so that we can edit, compile, and run it.*

Once blink.c is opened in Geany, you'll see the C code written to blink an LED, like the code we wrote in Python as shown in Figure 5-14. As you can see, the syntax for C is slightly more involved than Python. However, if you've ever used an Arduino for projects then it will look familiar to you (with some variations since Arduino code is not a direct port of C).

Figure 5-14. *Blink.c opened in Geany*

In looking at the code structure, the first thing that stands out is that as we did with Python, we're including libraries at the start of the script. The first is `<stdio.h>`, which is the input and output library that is standard to the C and C++ languages. The second library is `<wiringPi.h>`, which allows for communication between C and the GPIO pins and as previously mentioned is ported from the Raspberry Pi boards. And speaking of the GPIO pins, the first line of code after the library imports is the definition of the LED GPIO pin as pin 0. Of course, we aren't counting the physical GPIO pins in binary, so which pin is pin 0?

You may remember at the beginning of the Python section that we discussed how there were two numbering conventions for the GPIO pins that you could use with the Python library: the physical board numbers or the numbers that were dependent on the SoC's pinout control. wiringPi has its own additional numbering convention that is separate from both the physical numbers and the SoC's numbers and has to be used when coding in C on the Tinker Board. This is, of course, very confusing and a bit convoluted. However, there is a quick reference available that was also mentioned in a note at the beginning of the Python section where you can type sudo gpio readall into the terminal and it will give you a quick reference chart where you can easily see how all of these GPIO pin numbers correspond to each other, as shown in Figure 5-15. It's recommended to keep a separate terminal window open with this chart up as reference until you get used to the wiringPi numbering conventions or refer to Figure 5-15.

```
                    linaro@tinkerboard: ~/gpio_lib_python/test              _ □ ×
File  Edit  Tabs  Help
^Clinaro@tinkerboard:~/gpio_lib_python/test$ sudo gpio readall
+-----+-----+----------+------+---+--Tinker--+---+------+----------+-----+-----+
| CPU | wPi |   Name   | Mode | V | Physical | V | Mode |   Name   | wPi | CPU |
+-----+-----+----------+------+---+----++----+---+------+----------+-----+-----+
|     |     |   3.3v   |      |   |  1 || 2  |   |      | 5v       |     |     |
| 252 |  8  |   SDA.1  |      | 1 |  3 || 4  |   |      | 5V       |     |     |
| 253 |  9  |   SCL.1  |      | 1 |  5 || 6  |   |      | 0v       |     |     |
|  17 |  7  | GPIO0C1  | IN   | 1 |  7 || 8  | 1 | SERL | TxD1     | 15  | 161 |
|     |     |   0v     |      |   |  9 || 10 | 1 | SERL | RxD1     | 16  | 160 |
| 164 |  0  | GPIO5B4  | OUT  | 1 | 11 || 12 | 1 |      | GPIO6A0  |  1  | 184 |
| 166 |  2  | GPIO5B6  | SERL | 1 | 13 || 14 |   |      | 0v       |     |     |
| 167 |  3  | GPIO5B7  | SERL | 1 | 15 || 16 | 1 | IN   | GPIO5B2  |  4  | 162 |
|     |     |   3.3v   |      |   | 17 || 18 | 1 | IN   | GPIO5B3  |  5  | 163 |
| 257 | 12  | MOSI1    |      | 0 | 19 || 20 |   |      | 0v       |     |     |
| 256 | 13  | MISO1    |      | 1 | 21 || 22 | 0 | IN   | GPIO5C3  |  6  | 171 |
| 254 | 14  | SCLK1    |      | 1 | 23 || 24 | 1 |      | CE0      | 10  | 255 |
|     |     |   0v     |      |   | 25 || 26 | 1 |      | CE1      | 11  | 251 |
| 233 | 30  | SDA.2    | IN   | 1 | 27 || 28 | 1 |      | SCL.2    | 31  | 234 |
| 165 | 21  | GPIO5B5  | IN   | 1 | 29 || 30 |   |      | 0v       |     |     |
| 168 | 22  | GPIO5C0  | IN   | 1 | 31 || 32 | 1 | SERL | GPIO7C7  | 26  | 239 |
| 238 | 23  | GPIO7C6  | SERL | 1 | 33 || 34 |   |      | 0v       |     |     |
| 185 | 24  | GPIO6A1  |      | 0 | 35 || 36 | 1 | SERL | GPIO7A7  | 27  | 223 |
| 224 | 25  | GPIO7B0  | SERL | 1 | 37 || 38 | 1 |      | GPIO6A3  | 28  | 187 |
|     |     |   0v     |      |   | 39 || 40 | 0 |      | GPIO6A4  | 29  | 188 |
+-----+-----+----------+------+---+----++----+---+------+----------+-----+-----+
| CPU | wPi |   Name   | Mode | V | Physical | V | Mode |   Name   | wPi | CPU |
+-----+-----+----------+------+---+--Tinker--+---+------+----------+-----+-----+
linaro@tinkerboard:~/gpio_lib_python/test$ █
```

Figure 5-15. *The GPIO numbering sequences as seen after entering* sudo gpio readall *into the terminal*

Looking at the chart, we can see that wiringPi pin 0 is the equivalent to physical pin 11, so if you still have your breadboard assembled from earlier, you won't have to change any of your wiring for the LED circuit. It can remain in the same state shown in Figure 5-4 earlier.

Going back to the example code for blink.c that we have open in Geany, the next section after the pin declarations is the loop, which in C begins with int main (void), making it the equivalent to Python's try:. We aren't going to edit this code's main portions, since it's a simple and functional blink script. However, we should edit what it's going to print to the terminal, since in its current state it's referencing the Raspberry Pi. Let's edit it so that it will print the correct name:

```
printf ("Tinker Board blink\n")
```

Edit that line and then save it. Now we can compile the code and run it. Since we're using Geany, we can do everything from within its window, including tasks that would have required a separate terminal window; if you look at the bottom of the Geany window you can see that there is a Terminal option, as shown previously in Figure 5-14.

First, though, we need to compile blink.c; to do that, click the Compile button in the top menu bar of Geany, which has a blue pyramid with a yellow arrow pointing at a red circle as shown in Figure 5-16.

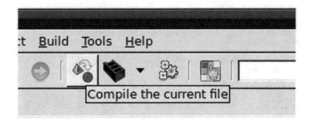

Figure 5-16. *The GUI button to compile in Geany*

After you click it, the Compiler at the bottom of the window will open and display a message that the "Compilation finished successfully" if there were no issues with your code, as shown in Figure 5-17. The next step is to build your code into an executable file with the terminal.

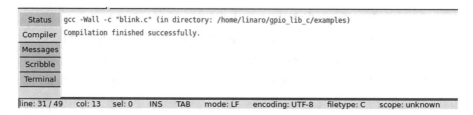

Figure 5-17. *The message after a successful code compilation*

Click the Terminal tab at the bottom of the Geany window and change directories to the examples folder within the C GPIO library folder by entering cd /home/linaro/gpio_lib_c/examples. Then enter gcc -o blink blink.c -lwiringPi to build the file. This will not return any message; in fact, it's successful if nothing is returned. Once the file is built it can be executed with sudo ./blink. Our line "Tinker Board blink" should print once in the terminal, as shown in Figure 5-18, and your LED should be blinking regularly. To end the script, much as we did with Python, you can type Control + C in the terminal and it will end.

```
Status     linaro@tinkerboard:~$ cd /home/linaro/gpio_lib_c/examples
           linaro@tinkerboard:~/gpio_lib_c/examples$ gcc -o blink blink.c -lwiringPi
Compiler   linaro@tinkerboard:~/gpio_lib_c/examples$ sudo ./blink
           Tinker Board blink
Messages   ^C
Scribble   linaro@tinkerboard:~/gpio_lib_c/examples$ sudo ./blink
           Tinker Board blink
Terminal   ^C
           linaro@tinkerboard:~/gpio_lib_c/examples$ █
line: 31 / 49   col: 13   sel: 0   INS   TAB   mode: LF   encoding: UTF-8   filetype: C   scope: unknown
```

Figure 5-18. *Blink.c running via the terminal in Geany*

Button in C

Much like the way we progressed with Python, let's add a button to our LED circuit and code in C. We're going to set up the same circuit that we did previously, connecting one lead from the button to the ground rail and the other lead to GPIO pin 13 as shown in Figure 5-8.

For the code, rather than editing the Blink example sketch we're going to start from scratch to get a better feel for how the C programming language works and the dependencies that are necessary to write programs for the Tinker Board's GPIO pins. Example code is great since you can run it without worry, but you really aren't learning anything by just executing pre-written scripts.

To start, we need to include those two libraries that we saw at the beginning of the Blink.c sketch:

```
#include <stdio.h>
#include <wiringPi.h>
```

You can always tell a library in C because it will be enclosed with < and > end with .h. Next, we're going to define our two GPIO pins using the wiringPi numbering scheme. We established with Blink.c that physical pin 11 is equivalent to wiringPi pin 0, and if we reference the chart in Figure 5-15, we can see that wiringPi pin 2 is the equivalent to physical pin 13, the pin we've been using for the button. Let's call the pins LED and BUTTON, respectively, with this code:

```
#define LED 0
#define BUTTON 2
```

Now we're ready for the loop. We'll need to include the wiringPi setup call to initialize the library and then set the LED as an output and the BUTTON as an input, since the LED is receiving data from the Tinker Board and the button is sending data into it. Then we'll begin the loop with a while statement.

In C, we can have the loop run infinitely, similar to Python, by using while(1), as that is the equivalent to Python's while True:. This is different from the parameter used in Blink.c, which was for (;;), and gives you another option to use going forward with your projects. In the loop we're going to again use an if/else statement so that when the button is pressed, the LED will turn on, and if the button is not pressed it will turn off. To close the loop in C, after beginning with while(1), we'll put in return 0; and the entire loop will look like this:

```
int main (void)
{
        wiringPiSetup();

        pinMode(LED, OUTPUT);
        pinMode(BUTTON, INPUT);

        while(1) {
                if (digitalRead(BUTTON) == 0) {
                digitalWrite(LED, HIGH);
                }
        else {
                digitalWrite(LED, LOW);
                }
        }
        return 0;
}
```

Note   Notice the syntax differences between C and Python. In the same way that indentations and colons are important in Python, curly brackets, semicolons and parenthesis are very important in C. Always check to make sure that you have closed sets of curly brackets and have semicolons placed appropriately at the ends of lines. Indentations in C are not related to syntax but are used to keep the code neat and readable.

Your entire script once combined should be structured like this:

```
#include <stdio.h>
#include <wiringPi.h>

#define LED 0
#define BUTTON 2

int main (void)
{
        wiringPiSetup();

        pinMode(LED, OUTPUT);
        pinMode(BUTTON, INPUT);

        while(1) {
                if (digitalRead(BUTTON) == 0) {
                digitalWrite(LED, HIGH);
                }
        else {
                digitalWrite(LED, LOW);
                }
        }
        return 0;
}
```

Now save your program in the examples folder of gpio_lib_c as button.c and follow the steps outlined earlier to compile, build, and execute your new script to control an LED with a button. Just as before, you can also substitute a switch for a button for a more permanent lighting solution following the circuit diagram shown earlier in Figure 5-9.

Note   If you do not include ".c" at the end of your program name when saving, Geany will not recognize it as a program written in C, and as a result you will not be able to compile.

Pulse Width Modulation

A common hardware programming concept that we have not discussed yet is Pulse Width Modulation (PWM), which enables you to control components in a way that resembles analog control. It's similar to what we explored with the photocell resistor, but using digital controls rather than a hardware workaround.

As we've discussed, the GPIO pins utilizing digital methods can be either on or off. PWM takes advantage of this by sending an on signal for a certain portion of time to the pin and then turning the pin off for a certain portion of time so that it pulses continuously in this pattern. The amount of time that the pin is on is referred to as the *pulse width*, and different patterns are referred to as *duty cycles*, described in percentages. For example, a 100% duty cycle would have the pin on for 100% of a measured time period, and a 25% duty cycle would have the pin on for 25% of a measured time period.

There are two types of PWM: hardware-controlled PWM and software-controlled PWM. The difference between the two is that hardware-controlled PWM has the duty cycle and bit toggling (on or off signal) controlled via the hardware on the board, while software-controlled PWM has everything controlled via the software. On the Tinker Board there are three pins that allow for hardware-controlled PWM: physical GPIO pins 32 and 33 and a third standalone PWM pin located between the USB ports and the Ethernet port. To use that third pin, you will have to solder directly to the Tinker Board, since it does not come with a header included.

To use PWM on any of the other GPIO pins, you will have to use software-controlled PWM. There is a library included in wiringPi for software-controlled PWM, though, so it can be done. First, let's look at how hardware-controlled PWM is implemented in C on the Tinker Board.

Coding with Hardware-Controlled PWM

As we saw with our original Blink example in C, there is a prewritten hardware-controlled PWM example in the examples folder that comes with the C library. It is simply called pwm.c. Locate this file in the examples folder inside the gpio_lib_c folder and open it in Geany, as shown in Figure 5-19.

```
pwm.c    softPWM.c
 6      *********************************************************************
 7      * This file is part of wiringPi:
 8      *   https://projects.drogon.net/raspberry-pi/wiringpi/
 9      *
10      *    wiringPi is free software: you can redistribute it and/or modify
11      *    it under the terms of the GNU Lesser General Public License as published by
12      *    the Free Software Foundation, either version 3 of the License, or
13      *    (at your option) any later version.
14      *
15      *    wiringPi is distributed in the hope that it will be useful,
16      *    but WITHOUT ANY WARRANTY; without even the implied warranty of
17      *    MERCHANTABILITY or FITNESS FOR A PARTICULAR PURPOSE.  See the
18      *    GNU Lesser General Public License for more details.
19      *
20      *    You should have received a copy of the GNU Lesser General Public License
21      *    along with wiringPi.  If not, see <http://www.gnu.org/licenses/>.
22      *********************************************************************
23      */
24
25     #include <wiringPi.h>
26
27     #include <stdio.h>
28     #include <stdlib.h>
29     #include <stdint.h>
30
31     int main (void)
32     {
33       int bright ;
34
35       printf ("Raspberry Pi wiringPi PWM test program\n") ;
36       wiringPiSetup();
37       pinMode (26, PWM_OUTPUT) ;
38       for (;;)
39       {
40         for (bright = 0 ; bright < 1024 ; bright=bright+4)
41         {
42           pwmWrite (26, bright) ;
43           delay (10) ;
44         }
45
46         for (bright = 1023 ; bright >= 0 ; bright=bright-4)
47         {
48           pwmWrite (26, bright) ;
49           delay (10) ;
50         }
51       }
52
53       return 0 ;
54     }
55
```

Figure 5-19. *The included hardware PWM example code entitled pwm.c*

Again, we can see that much like the included Blink example, it is a direct port from the Raspberry Pi, with a line set to print to the terminal referencing the Pi before the loop begins. Just as we did with the Blink.c example, edit the line so that it reads:

```
printf ("Tinker Board wiringPi PWM test program\n");
```

There are two more libraries included at the top that we haven't seen yet in C; <stdlib.h> and <stdint.h>. Both are C libraries; <stdlib.h> is a general utilities library, and <stdint.h> is an integers library. Both are needed for the increased software needs for PWM.

The loop is set up with the integer bright acting as a placeholder for the pulse width value. There are two for loops inside the main loop. The first increases the pulse width incrementally, which will have the LED steadily increase in brightness until it reaches the maximum brightness possible. The second decreases the pulse width incrementally, which will make the LED steadily fade until it is completely off. The value of 1024 expressed in the for loops is the maximum analog value in the C programming language, which is used since PWM is imitating analog behavior.

The final important note about this program is the pin that the LED is attached to. Since this is a hardware-controlled PWM example, we'll need to attach the LED to one of the hardware PWM GPIO pins. The pin used in the example is wiringPi pin 26, which corresponds to physical pin 32 as seen previously in Figure 5-15, by referencing gpio readall in the terminal.

Keep the same LED circuit that we've been working with and attach the positive lead to physical pin 32, as shown in Figure 5-20.

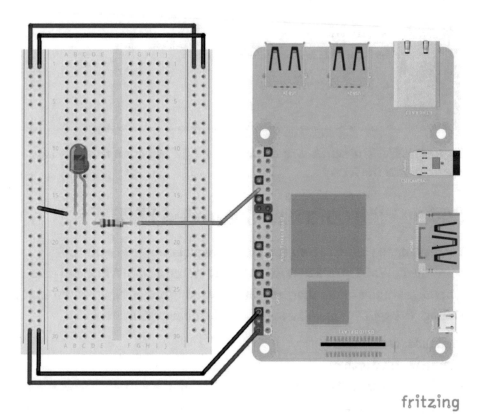

Figure 5-20. *The circuit diagram for attaching the LED to GPIO physical pin 32 for hardware-controlled PWM*

After this, compile the program as we've been doing and execute it via the terminal. The line "Tinker Board wiringPi PWM test program" should print to the terminal, as shown in Figure 5-21, and your LED should fade smoothly on and off continuously.

123

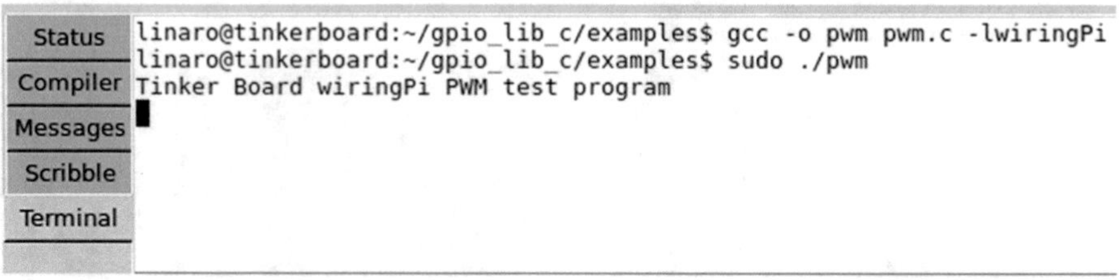

```
Status    linaro@tinkerboard:~/gpio_lib_c/examples$ gcc -o pwm pwm.c -lwiringPi
          linaro@tinkerboard:~/gpio_lib_c/examples$ sudo ./pwm
Compiler  Tinker Board wiringPi PWM test program
Messages  ▮
Scribble
Terminal
```

Figure 5-21. The hardware-controlled PWM test code running via the terminal in Geany

Coding with Software-Controlled PWM

We're going to write our own code to create an example of software-controlled PWM. Open a new file in Geany, name it softPWM.c and save it in the examples folder that we've been working out of. Now we can start coding. To begin, we're going to import the following libraries:

```
#include <stdint.h>
#include <stdio.h>
#include <stdlib.h>

#include <wiringPi.h>
#include <softPwm.h>
```

The first three libraries are the general C libraries that we've been working with, followed by the wiringPi library and then a new library to us: <softPwm.h>, which is the software PWM library for use with wiringPi. This will allow us to use some special software PWM functions in our code to streamline our program.

Next, we'll begin our main loop and declare our variables as well as initialize wiringPi, which will look like this:

```
int main (void) {
        int LED = 0;
        int i;
        wiringPiSetup();
```

LED is going to symbolize the GPIO pin that our LED is attached to. Again, you can use any GPIO pin for software PWM, but let's stick with GPIO physical pin 11, which is wiringPi's pin 0, since we've been using it throughout this chapter. The variable int i is going to act as the place holder for the pulse width value, much as bright did in the hardware PWM example that we just looked at.

Next, we'll do some further setup for the LED's GPIO pin so that software PWM will be able to control it. First, we'll set it as an output with this statement:

```
pinMode (LED, PWM_OUTPUT);
```

Then we'll set it up as a PWM pin with this:

```
softPwmCreate (LED, 0, 100);
```

The softPwmCreate command takes three arguments; the first is the pin that will be set up for software PWM. Next is the minimum pulse width value that will be received via the software. Here we have that as 0, or off. Finally, the third parameter is the maximum pulse width value that will be received. 100 is best practice for use with the library. Unlike the hardware PWM example that utilized the true analog maximum value of 1024, the wiringPi software PWM works best with a maximum value of 100, since it is completely digital dependent.

After the setup is the main loop, which is begun with

```
while(1) {
```

Just as in the hardware PWM example, we'll be using two for loops, one that will increase the pulse width value and thus the brightness of the LED and one that will decrease the pulse width value to dim the LED so that it turns off. Using a maximum value of 100 and int i, the for loops will be set up like this:

```
for (i = 0; i < 100; i++)
{
softPwmWrite (LED, i);
delay(10);
}

for (i = 100; i >= 0; i--)
{
softPwmWrite (LED, i);
delay(10);
}
```

We'll end our loop with return 0; and our entire program should look like this once complete:

```
#include <stdint.h>
#include <stdio.h>
#include <stdlib.h>

#include <wiringPi.h>
#include <softPwm.h>

int main (void) {
        int LED = 0;
        int i;

        wiringPiSetup();

        pinMode (LED, PWM_OUTPUT);
        softPwmCreate (LED, 0, 100);

        while (1) {
                for (i = 0; i < 100; i++)
                {
                softPwmWrite (LED, i);
                delay(10);
```

```
        }
        for (i = 100; i >= 0; i--)
        {
        softPwmWrite (LED, i);
        delay(10);
        }
    }
    return 0;
}
```

Return the LED's positive lead to GPIO physical pin 11, as previously shown in Figure 5-4, and then compile and execute the softPWM.c program. As in the hardware PWM example, your LED should be smoothly fading on and off continuously.

Note   Both hardware and software PWM are available in the Python library as well.

The Lack of a Real Time Clock

Now that we've gone over some basic hardware programming with the GPIO pins, you may be thinking that using a single-board computer for your hardware project needs is the best way to go. At first glance, the benefits in doing this are overwhelmingly positive. You can use multiple programming languages, the board is running a full version of Linux, and the SoC's CPU is much more powerful than most microcontroller boards, such as an Arduino. But despite these advantages, there is one very important feature that SBCs running Linux lack that almost all microcontroller boards have: a real time clock.

A real time clock is very important for programming hardware components. It allows everything to work as expected and to run smoothly; especially with things like PWM which could be controlling motors or other components whose proper operation depends on receiving the correct timing instructions.

When programming hardware on an SBC running Linux, we control the clock purely through software. This works, as you've just seen with all the examples, but it will never be as dependable in the long term as a microcontroller or in situations that require precise timings, such as motor control. This also eats up CPU resources with the SoC. In fact, for every pin that you run software PWM on the Tinker Board you'll notice a CPU usage increase between 10 and 20%. With all this in mind, when should you use the GPIO pins on the Tinker Board or other SBCs?

As discussed at the very beginning of this book, it's the features of a full desktop operating system, Internet connectivity, processing power, and much more that make SBCs so useful. The GPIO pins are a bonus to these main features and as a result are not the focus of what these boards can offer. They should be used to compliment a project or when using a traditional microcontroller board will be more cumbersome.

Examples include when a specialized operating system that focuses on a specific task, such as game emulation or file management, will be in use and requires a few shortcut buttons to easily navigate rather than keeping a keyboard hooked up. Or when sensors will be reading data that will be logged and require storage to eventually be published on a social media page. These are just a few projects that could see the benefit of an SBC with GPIO pins.

You can see why if you just wanted to blink a few LEDs you will probably be better off using a microcontroller rather than an SBC. We'll be going over a few project options in the third part of this book that will further demonstrate when an SBC, and specifically the Tinker Board, is the best choice for a project.

Wrapping Things Up

In this chapter we were able to gain an understanding of how the GPIO pins on the Tinker Board work with both the Python and C libraries. We also discussed the best use case scenarios for implementing the GPIO pins in a project on an SBC such as the Tinker Board. We'll be building on this basic knowledge during the projects portion of this book. But first, there is one additional operating system from ASUS for the Tinker Board to explore: Android!

CHAPTER 6

Android on the Tinker Board

In addition to TinkerOS, ASUS has another official operating system for the Tinker Board: Android. It can be easy to forget that Android is actually an open source operating system based on Linux. As a result, anyone can build their own distribution of it, just as with desktop Linux distributions such as Debian.

At the time of writing, the version of Android that ASUS has released for the Tinker Board is based on Android version 7, known as Nougat. Although an older version, it is still supported and receives security updates, making it a safe operating system to use connected to the Internet.

Installation

To prep your SD card or eMMC to install and run Android, you'll follow the instructions outlined in Chapter 3, with the only difference being that you will download the Android .img file from the ASUS Tinker Board website rather than TinkerOS. After you've followed the steps, you can try booting into Android. The first boot into Android takes longer than subsequent boots before you finally reach the desktop because of the file systems being built. Subsequent boots are much faster and only take between 10 to 20 seconds.

© Liz Clark 2019
L. Clark, *Practical Tinker Board*, https://doi.org/10.1007/978-1-4842-3826-4_6

Note   If you get any errors on the first boot, such as a disk repair error, let it repair itself and see if it boots successfully afterward. If it doesn't, try imaging your storage again or using a different SD card.

Navigation

Once you get to the Android landing page, you'll notice that it looks similar to an Android tablet interface, complete with the message to "swipe up" to enter the homepage. If you're using a screen with touch capabilities, you can plug the USB from your monitor into the Tinker Board and treat it like a tablet. If you prefer to use a keyboard and mouse, though, you can still do that.

Try to think of the mouse acting as a touch input. Every time you left-click, it's like you've tapped the screen; and if you need to swipe in a certain direction, you'll hold down the left button and move the mouse in the correct direction. You may experience some glitches using this method, though, as the mouse can become very sensitive compared to the inputs that the Android system is expecting from a touch input.

You can also use a remote, whether a traditional TV-style remote or gamepad, to navigate as well, like operating a Smart TV or other similar device. Since Android is set up to be a touchscreen operating system, a remote works very well for navigation. The remote can use a wireless dongle or Bluetooth (BLE) to communicate with the Tinker Board. These remotes are sold for home theater solutions or you can get adventurous and build your own using a development board that has BLE available onboard. We'll be discussing remote control options with the Tinker Board during the project chapters as well, including how to build a quick and easy BLE DIY remote.

The Home Screen

Now that you've chosen how you're going to navigate Android, let's look at the default home screen provided by ASUS. As shown in Figure 6-1, in the top-right corner there is a battery status icon as well as a clock, like an Android phone display. Moving toward the middle of the screen there is an icon for the Contacts app and then right below that, from left to right, are the Email, Internet Browser, Apps Menu, Music App, Photos and Camera apps. We'll explore the functionality of some of these apps shortly.

Figure 6-1. *The Android landing page on the Tinker Board*

At the very bottom of the screen are navigation and utility controls. From left to right they are the Lower Volume, Back, Home, Overview, and Raise Volume buttons. For those unfamiliar with Android, the Back button will bring you back one page in an app, the Home button will usually bring you back to the home screen, and the Overview button will show you which apps are currently open. You can then quickly switch between apps or close apps out.

More Apps

There are more preinstalled applications in this Android distro than appear on the home page. If you go to the Apps Menu icon, it will open a new window which reveals all the apps that are currently installed, as shown in Figure 6-2. As you can see, the apps are standard Android and utility apps that you would expect to find after a fresh installation of an operating system. A lot of these apps will function best with an Internet connection available, so let's connect to Wi-Fi and then come back to explore.

Figure 6-2. *The preinstalled apps for Android on the Tinker Board*

Connecting to Wi-Fi

To have the full Android experience, it's important to get your Tinker Board online, especially considering that Android usually runs on a device with data communication enabled. Since we discussed security in the TinkerOS chapter, you may be wondering about security for this Android distro, especially since it's an older Android version. At the time of writing,

Android Nougat is still supported by Android. It still gets security patches, and if you look in the release notes from ASUS they do note when they've implemented a security patch, so if you don't do anything sketchy you'll have a secure experience. With all this in mind, let's navigate to Settings and connect to your network.

Note   You can, of course, use wired Internet via the Tinker Board's onboard Ethernet port, but depending on your router's location this may not be an option for you. If speed and stability are priorities for you when using Android for a project you have in mind, then of course use Ethernet.

After entering the Settings menu, you'll see that the first section at the top of the screen is Wireless & Networks, as shown in Figure 6-3. Click on Wi-Fi, which will bring you to a new screen. You'll see a toggle to turn Wi-Fi on or off. The default after a fresh installation is off, so make sure that you toggle it on to begin the connection process.

Figure 6-3. *Wireless and networks settings*

After you toggle Wi-Fi on, Android will say that it is searching for available networks to connect to. After a few seconds, all of the available networks will be listed, as shown in Figure 6-4. Select your network from the list and you'll then be prompted for a password for your network. After entering your password, Android will check your authentication and after a few moments, assuming you've entered your password correctly, it will say you are connected to your network. You'll also see the Wi-Fi symbol with a strength level indicator pop-up in the upper-right corner of your screen. This will allow you to quickly see if you're connected in the future and also check on signal strength depending on your location.

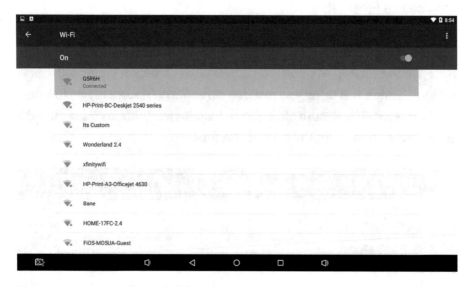

Figure 6-4. *List of available wireless networks that appears after you toggle Wi-Fi on*

More Settings

While we're in Settings, we might as well explore a bit. After finishing up with Wi-Fi, choose Back at the bottom of your screen to go back one page to the main Settings menu. Similar to other Android devices and iOS devices, it has settings options for Bluetooth, display, notifications, and so on. Some items here are a bit different, though, since they are set up for the Tinker Board and not for a mobile device. For example, as seen in Figure 6-3, there are additional Internet settings beyond Wi-Fi if you need them. Under the More button in Wireless & Networks there is a VPN option, which has become more common now for mainstream devices, but there are also Ethernet settings to check and configure as well.

Battery?

Moving down the Settings menu, you'll see a Battery section. In that section, you'll see an option to show the battery percentage. Any power source being used through the USB power port, whether it be a USB power supply or a portable battery bank, will show that the Tinker Board is "charging" and has a battery of 100% (Figure 6-5). Since this is an operating system for tablets and phones that have rechargeable batteries, and the Tinker Board does not have an onboard rechargeable battery, it will still show that the Tinker Board is "charging" and is at 100% when plugged into a wall outlet.

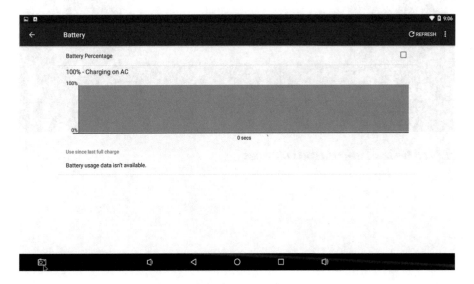

Figure 6-5. *The battery percentage screen*

HDMI and Audio Source

One of the more important sections in Settings for the Tinker Board is the ability to select your audio and video inputs and outputs. If you navigate to the HDMI and Audio Source section, you'll be able to choose your preferred options; such as audio traveling through HDMI or the headphone jack (Figure 6-6). Here you can also adjust the screen resolution, screen settings for zoom, and a timeout setting that sets a timer for when the screen will go to sleep, similar to energy settings on your laptop or desktop computer. All of these settings will be very important if you plan to use Android for media playback.

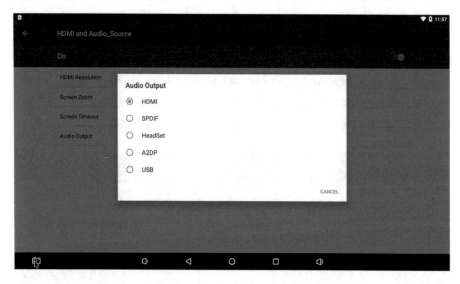

Figure 6-6. *Audio output choices*

Turning on Developer Options

The last major setting that we're going to walk through is turning on Developer Options. Finding it is a bit of an Android Easter egg, since it isn't as simple as toggling something on or off. Scroll down to the very bottom of the settings page and click About Tablet. Once on that page, find the Build number section at the bottom of the screen. There you'll see the current build number for the version of Android that you're running on the Tinker Board. Now click the build number five times. A counter should pop up on the screen giving you a countdown to how many more clicks are required to enter developer mode. Once you've enabled it, it will say "You are now a developer!" on the screen, as shown in Figure 6-7.

Figure 6-7. *"You are now a developer!"*

Now go back to the main settings page and you'll see a new option in System Settings, called Developer Options. Click it and you'll see a lot of options that are a bit unusual to have access to. Most are for testing purposes for, you guessed it, Android developers. But a lot of them can be fun to play around with for more advanced users, such as enabling a Bluetooth snoop log, bug reports, and forcing GPU rendering to name a few. If you decide that you don't want these settings enabled, you can toggle them off at the top of the page. Doing this doesn't make the Developer Options entry in Settings disappear, though. After you enable it the first time, it will remain an option to toggle off and on in Settings going forward.

More to Explore

There are, of course, more settings available to you, but most users will more than likely find Wi-Fi and audio and video settings to be the most important, as well as Developer options for more advanced users (and hopefully you got a good chuckle out of the Battery setting's readout). Feel free to explore and change any settings according to your preferences. We're going to move on from Settings and go back to the apps.

Apps In-Depth

Now that you're online and you have your other settings sorted out, let's take a closer look at some of the applications available. We'll look at how to use some of the more unique apps and the functionality available within them that can help you get the most out of Android on the Tinker Board.

Camera

The Camera app allows you to take photos with a ribbon cable camera module or USB webcam. The camera module can be connected to the onboard MIPI CSI camera connector, which is located next to the HDMI port. The USB webcam would of course be plugged into one of the USB ports. We're going to explore connecting a camera module to the MIPI connector for the purpose of walking through the app's functionality.

There are many different cameras available that will be compatible with the MIPI connector from a variety of companies. You can go the route of a basic camera module or one with special features, such as a night vision camera or one that has interchangeable lenses. The classic ribbon cable cameras from the Raspberry Pi Foundation are also compatible, so if you have been doing Raspberry Pi projects and have a camera module then you can use that hardware with the Tinker Board.

To connect the camera, first locate the plug on the Tinker Board as shown in Figure 6-8, and gently lift-up the white plastic bar. This will eventually hold the ribbon cable in place.

Figure 6-8.   *The camera module plug. Notice the camera icon directly above it on the Tinker Board's PCB.*

Next, take your camera module and locate the exposed pins on the ribbon cable. The pins will be shiny in appearance and will need to make contact with the pins inside the plug on the board. Carefully insert the ribbon cable with the pins facing toward the HDMI port as shown in Figure 6-9. After you're sure that the ribbon cable cannot be inserted any further, gently push down on the white lever on the plug to secure the camera's cable in place.

Figure 6-9. *A camera module's ribbon cable plugged into the Tinker Board. Notice that the cable's contact pins are facing toward the HDMI port's side of the camera connector.*

Note   Both the ribbon cable connector and ribbon cable are fragile and need to be handled with care during installation and use. They also tend to be sensitive to static. Be aware of any strain that is placed on the ribbon cable while in use and consider a case or mount for the camera module and its cable for long term use.

After your camera is plugged into the socket, open the Camera app. You should see a message that the camera is being set up. After a few seconds it should recognize that the camera module is connected to your board and you should see what the camera is seeing displayed on screen as shown in Figure 6-10.

Figure 6-10. *The default Camera app GUI*

Note   If it says that the Camera app has stopped or that there is an error in connecting to the camera module, then the camera is not connected correctly. Try reseating the ribbon cable or checking that the ribbon cable is plugged into the socket in the correct orientation.

Camera App Functionality

The Camera app has basic functionality with a minimalist interface. You can take a picture by clicking on the camera icon located on the right side of the screen. You can also adjust flash, bring a grid overlay onto the viewfinder for optimally framed photos, and set a timer to delay by either 3 or 10 seconds when the picture will be taken after you press the button to take the picture. All of the photos that you take will be saved in the Gallery app, as shown in Figure 6-11. In addition to the preinstalled Camera app there are more apps you can use with a connected camera that provide additional functionality and features. We'll look at an app that does this in a little bit.

Figure 6-11.   *The Gallery app. All photos are sorted via the application they were taken with.*

Music and Video

One of the appealing features of the Android operating system on the Tinker Board is the ability to be a small, compact media player for your video and audio files. Let's take a look at the built-in apps that come preinstalled and some others that you may enjoy.

The Music App

The preinstalled Music app is a robust player with a straightforward and well-organized GUI. There are tabs for Artists, Albums, Songs, Playlists and Now Playing. Clicking the option button (...) in the bottom-right corner brings up the options Party shuffle and Shuffle all. The difference between the two is that Party shuffle creates a playlist of songs of the same genre so that you can see what is going to be played next and add songs in or take songs out of rotation, whereas Shuffle all is completely random.

If you connect any external storage via USB that has audio files on it, the Music app will automatically find them and sort them according to the files' metadata. As long as your metadata is correct, you will see all of your albums and artists as shown in Figure 6-12.

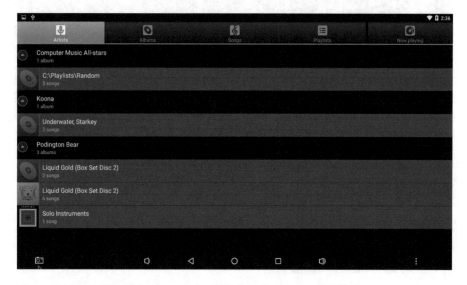

Figure 6-12. *The Music app's GUI for artists and albums*

The Video App

The preinstalled Video app is a bit barebones. Available video files appear in a list, and selecting one allows it to play. As you saw with the Music app, if you connect a flash drive with videos on it, they will appear in the queue for playback. You can also review videos that you record with the Camera app, as shown in Figure 6-13. This app gets the basic job done; but if you're looking for a GUI to similar the Music app's and more options in general, consider the VLC Media Player for Android.

Figure 6-13. *The preinstalled Video app's playback screen*

Installing VLC

You may remember that we installed VLC during the TinkerOS chapter. Again, it's a great open source media player and it's available for Android as a download directly from VLC.

To download the VLC APK file, open the browser and navigate to the VLC download page for Android.[1] Once there, you'll click the "download the APK package from our mirrors" link underneath the Google Play and Amazon Fire App store icons, as shown in Figure 6-14.

Figure 6-14. *The VLC for Android webpage. Notice the direct download link below the Google Play and Amazon Fire icons.*

This brings you to a new page with versions available for different ARM architectures (Figure 6-15).

---

[1]videolan.org/vlc/download-android.html

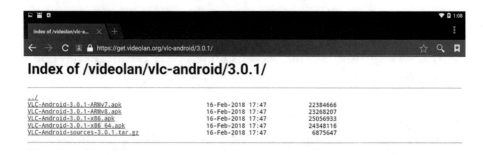

Figure 6-15. *The available VLC downloads for Android. Be sure to select ARMv7.*

Select and download the ARMv7 version; as you may remember from Chapter 1, that is the Rockchip architecture version on the Tinker Board. A few seconds after you click, VLC should begin downloading. Once it finishes, you'll get a notification at the top of your screen. If you click that notification, you'll be prompted to install VLC. Before you do this, though, you'll need to ensure that you have enabled installations for apps from unknown sources. You can toggle this option on or off by going to Settings ➤ Security ➤ Unknown Sources in the Device administration section. After that, click Install on the VLC notification and after it finishes, an option to launch VLC will pop up on your screen. Click to launch and VLC will open.

After opening it the first time you'll be asked to allow it permission to access photos, media, and other files on your device. Click Allow, especially since it is a media player.

Using VLC

Like the default Music app, VLC can find video and audio files that are located on external storage devices. When you first attach a USB drive with VLC, you'll be asked if you want to import the media stored on it, as shown in Figure 6-16. After a few moments, your videos and audio files will populate and be sorted according to their metadata.

Figure 6-16. *Attaching external storage in VLC*

All videos will play full screen; and if you're using a mouse to navigate, mouse functionality will not be available during playback. This is an idiosyncrasy that pops up from time to time when using a keyboard and mouse with Android. You can pause and resume playback by hitting the space bar on your keyboard and exit playback to the main GUI by hitting Esc. After a video ends, you will be automatically brought back to the main GUI as well.

Audio files can be sorted by artist, album, songs, genre or playlists. If you play music in an album, the entire track listing will remain on the screen, and the song that is currently playing will appear at the bottom of the screen with pause and play buttons located in the bottom-right corner as shown in Figure 6-17. The track currently playing will also remain visible if you travel to other pages in VLC.

Figure 6-17. *Now playing in VLC*

An additional feature is that music will continue to play in the background when using other apps, as with desktop music players. With the functionality available for both video and audio, VLC can be a single solution for media playback in Android on the Tinker Board, just like it was for TinkerOS.

ApkInstaller

One app that comes preinstalled may be unfamiliar to you, especially if you are not an avid Android user, and that is ApkInstaller. If you have no idea what that means, you can probably at least infer that it is an application that installs something, that something being an APK. But what is an APK?

An APK is the installation file for an Android app, similar to .EXE files on desktop machines. If you're following along with the examples, you actually just installed an APK for VLC. Traditionally, you would install an APK file, or app, through an app store; such as Google Play and as a result never even think about the fact that a file is being installed onto an operating system. ApkInstaller takes out that app store middle man and allows you to take an APK file and manually install it onto your Android operating system.

Legal Considerations

The idea of installing apps without an app store sounds very freeing and makes Android feel more like a desktop operating system. But if this is making you wonder if there are any piracy or legal concerns associated with this process, then you're absolutely right. If you were to download an app's APK from a third-party website, especially an app that would cost money if you were to download it from an app store, and install that APK and run it, that would certainly be considered piracy and could be subject to legal action. In general, it's ill-advised to download an APK file from a third-party site since there are virus concerns associated with many of them. So, with all of these red flag concerns in mind, why is this application included?

An ApkInstaller doesn't have to be used for technological evil. If you were to develop your own Android app and install its APK, that would be completely legal, and you would have every right to do this. Other scenarios could be if another developer sent you their APK to install and test, or perhaps a company were to post an APK file online, like VLC, for their app to install outside an app store environment. All of these are perfectly legal and sensible uses of the ApkInstaller, and they are why ASUS includes it. This version of Android for the Tinker Board is really intended for developers to have a high-powered test bed to play around in Android so that they don't have to have an emulator on their desktop or a phone or tablet.

How It Works

With all the disclaimers and background out of the way, we can go over how ApkInstaller works. First navigate to the ApkInstaller icon and launch it by clicking on it. The first time you open ApkInstaller, a message from Android lets you know that the app needs you to grant access to read from and write to external storage devices. This is so that external storage can be utilized by the app in case you are loading or saving APK files via USB storage devices. Allow the app to do this by clicking OK. Next, it will ask you to allow it to access photos, media and files on your device, an agreement similar to those often seen for Android apps. Select Allow to proceed. After the permissions have been set and the app opens, you'll see that it's a very simple GUI with buttons for Install, Manage, and Exit (Figure 6-18).

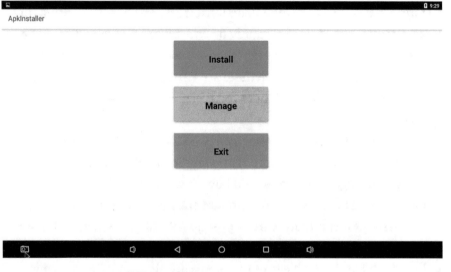

Figure 6-18. *The ApkInstaller GUI*

Install

If you have an APK file on your SD card, eMMC, or removable storage device that you want to install, use the Install button at the top. When you click Install, it brings you to a page that shows you the available storage devices connected to your Tinker Board, as shown in Figure 6-19. On the original Tinker Board, most apps, including ApkInstaller, consider the SD card to be the Internal Memory. It will almost never say SD card. Select your storage device and then navigate to the location of your APK file. Select the file and you'll be prompted to proceed with the installation by clicking Install. After a few moments, you'll receive confirmation that the file has finished installing with a pop-up window. You'll also have the option to open the app right away from that pop-up.

Figure 6-19. *Attached storage devices available to install APK files from*

Manage

The second option in ApkInstaller is Manage. By clicking the Manage
button, you're brought to a list of all the apps currently installed on your
Tinker Board. If you click an app, you'll be greeted by a menu with options
to Launch, Export, Uninstall, or Cancel, as shown in Figure 6-20. Selecting
Launch opens the app directly. Export exports the APK file for the app
that you can then store for later installation. Uninstall uninstalls the app
from your Tinker Board, and Cancel exits the Action menu. Another handy
feature on the Manage page is the ability to see the version number for
each app installed.

Figure 6-20. *Options available for apps when using the Manage tool*

Note   If you export any APK files, please keep the legal discussion
from earlier in the chapter in mind.

Exit

The last button available in ApkInstaller is Exit, and unlike its counterparts, it doesn't have any advanced features of functionality; it simply closes out the app.

But as you can see, the ApkInstaller app is quite powerful and really opens up the Android experience for developers. It does some things with a single click that can sometimes be nearly impossible or extremely difficult otherwise. But as discussed earlier, it's important to use this app for its intended purpose only and not to use it for malicious purposes.

Power

One of the most valuable functions in the apps menu is the Power button. Although not an app, it allows you to safely shut down and reboot the Tinker Board while in the Android operating system (Figure 6-21). Without it, there would be a risk of data corruption to your storage from unexpected shutdowns.

Figure 6-21. *The options for shutdown and reboot*

Where Is the App Store?

With all this talk about apps, you may have noticed that there is no app store preinstalled on this Android distro. Traditionally the app store that you would find on most Android phones or tablets is the Google Play store; so why isn't it on the Tinker Board? Again, this distro is meant for developers, but another reason is that in order for Google Play to run and be used on an Android device, it needs to be a certified Google Android device.

The Tinker Board is not a certified Google Android device, but there are other app stores available for Android that can be installed and used on the Tinker Board. The one that we're going to look at is F-Droid, which features free and open source applications to install. They also have automatic updates and security patches for their apps similar to what you may be familiar with on your smart phone or tablet's app store.

Note   There have been some success stories on the forums of getting the Google Play store running on the Tinker Board. However, the process has not worked consistently, and it is a bit of a hack. Additionally, since the Tinker Board is not a certified Google Android device at this time, this would be a violation of the Google Play terms of service. As a result, the process could not be showcased in this book. Therefore, we are instead looking at the open source option F-Droid.

Installing F-Droid

The installation process for F-Droid is a lot like what we did for VLC media player. First, we're going to navigate to F-Droid's web site.[2] Toward the middle of the F-Droid homepage (Figure 6-22), there is a Download F-Droid button. Clicking here will begin to download the APK file to your Tinker Board. After the download completes, a notification will appear at the top of your screen and prompt you to install the APK file. Click Install and after a minute or two the installation will finish, and a pop-up window will let you know that F-Droid has finished installing. From there you can click to open F-Droid.

Figure 6-22. *The F-Droid web page. Notice the download option toward the middle of the page.*

---

[2]f-droid.org

Exploring F-Droid

After opening F-Droid, you'll notice that the layout is very similar to other app stores with a landing page showcasing featured apps of different genres, as shown in Figure 6-23. The focus of F-Droid is to offer open source apps that appeal to the open source community, so there are many developer tools available here as well as apps featuring Tux as their icon mascot.

Figure 6-23. *The F-Droid app store's Categories view*

Almost every app genre is featured here, though, from audio players to Internet security to games. We're going to look at a couple of apps from F-Droid to fill in some gaps left by the absence of the Google Play store that some avid Android fans may be feeling.

Installing an app from F-Droid is very simple. Navigate to an app that you wish to install, and you'll see a button for Install (Figure 6-24). Click that, and the download process will begin. After the app has downloaded, you'll be asked if you want to install the app. Agree to the installation by clicking Install, and after a few seconds your app will be ready to use. A pop-up will ask if you'd like to launch the app. You can click Launch to go directly into the app or Cancel to continue browsing F-Droid.

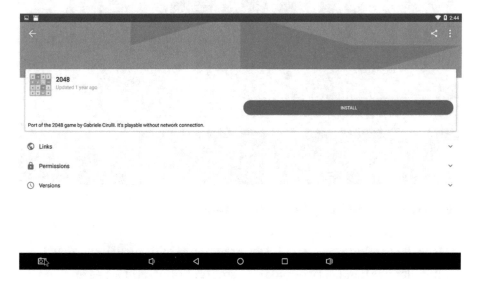

Figure 6-24. *How apps appear for installation in F-Droid*

As you can see, there are a wide variety of apps to choose from and try out in the F-Droid store. A few that many people may find particularly interesting are Newpipe, 2048, and Open Camera.

The Newpipe app is a YouTube player that pulls from YouTube in close to real time by showing you trending videos and having a search option that seems to be on par with what you would expect from the desktop site or an official app. You can also view videos in their full resolution and adjust video settings as needed as shown in Figure 6-25. Of course, you can view YouTube videos in the included Internet browser, but having a standalone app option can sometimes offer a better experience, especially on a mobile OS such as Android.

Figure 6-25. *The Newpipe video settings*

It really wouldn't be a mobile OS experience without games. 2048 is a game that has been very popular on smart phones, and it has an open source port to F-Droid (Figure 6-26). It's a numbers-based game and although you can play it with a mouse, serious players may want to hook up a touch screen for the full experience.

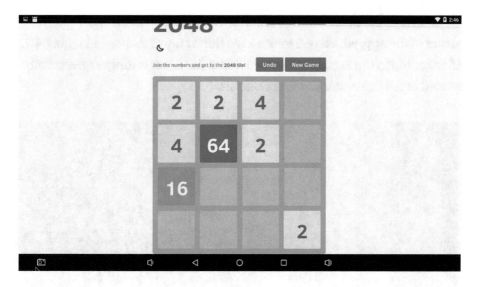

Figure 6-26. *2048 gameplay in action*

Media playback and games are great, but let's wrap this up with a look at a more functional app: Open Camera. Open Camera is a camera app that utilizes a camera attached to the Tinker Board just like the included Camera app in the Android distro. Open Camera is a much more robust camera app though, featuring many advanced controls, such as zoom, bitrate, and framerate controls for video and a customizable GUI.

Using Open Camera for Time-Lapses

One feature that really stands out for Open Camera is the timer. This allows you to set up a time-lapse camera with very little effort. Time-lapse camera projects with single-board computers are quite popular because of their size, processing power, and storage capabilities. Often this is done in a Linux operating system, like TinkerOS, but that requires programming and can be complicated depending on your needs. Using Open Camera with this Android distro, though, makes things simple and allows you to adjust settings easily if you need to through the GUI.

To access the timer settings, click the Settings icon in the top-right corner of the app, which resembles a machine cog, as shown in Figure 6-27. After getting to the Settings page, you'll find the timer settings conveniently located at the top under Camera Controls.

Figure 6-27. *The Open Camera GUI*

To set up a continuous time-lapse we'll first need to select how often we want a picture to be taken. Click the Timer option at the top of the page, which will have a menu with different time intervals, as shown in Figure 6-28. Select the option that makes the most sense for your time-lapse subject. Longer intervals are great for longer time-lapses, such as sunsets. Shorter intervals are ideal for things like project builds or 3D prints. After you've made your selection, this menu will minimize.

Figure 6-28. *The Timer options for time intervals*

Next, select how long your time-lapse will last by clicking the Repeat option. You'll see that there aren't as many options here, as shown in Figure 6-29. If you want to capture a quick time-lapse, then any of the 2X to 10X options will work well for you, but for anything longer than ten photos you'll want to select Unlimited. This means that the time-lapse will continue running until you stop it manually.

Figure 6-29. *The Repeat options. Unlimited will allow your time-lapses to go for as long as you want them to.*

The final step is to go to the Repeat mode interval option, as shown in Figure 6-30. You'll want this setting to match your Timer setting. For example, if you've selected 5 seconds for your Timer, then you'll choose 5 seconds for your Repeat mode interval. Otherwise, you may find that you're taking too many or too few photos in most cases. However, feel free to experiment for different effects and results.

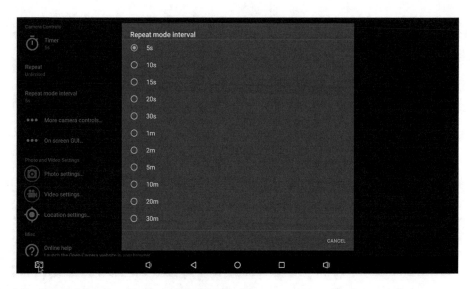

Figure 6-30. *Options available for the repeat mode interval*

After your settings are set up, return to the main Open Camera GUI, where you'll see your camera preview screen. To begin your time-lapse, you'll click the camera icon on the right side of the screen. Your time-lapse will begin and you'll see a countdown that matches your Timer interval that was set up in the previous steps, as shown in Figure 6-31. Now your time-lapse is running until you end it by clicking the camera icon again. After you end it, a small message will appear briefly on the screen that says "Cancelled timer." As you can see, this makes time lapses very simple to set up and configure to your needs. There are many more features within Open Camera, too many to go over in this chapter, but hopefully you now have an idea of what it has to offer when used on the Tinker Board and the possibilities of many of the apps available from F-Droid.

Figure 6-31.   The Open Camera GUI while a time-lapse is in progress. Notice the 3 over the preview window, which lets you know that a photo will be taken in 3 seconds.

Note   If you want to take a single photo with the app, then you'll have to reset your timer settings that were set up in the previous steps.

Conclusion

When we typically think of Android, we think of smart phones or tablets, usually with Google integration. Android for the Tinker Board is a departure from that and instead goes the open source route to give you an idea of what this OS architecture is capable of outside its branded smart phone and tablet form. At this time there aren't many single-board computers that have a dedicated Android operating system distributed by the manufacturer, so the Tinker Board provides a great opportunity to explore Android from a different perspective.

PART III

Tinker Board Projects

CHAPTER 7

Project 1: Build a Game Emulation System

We've spent the last few chapters getting acquainted with the Tinker Board, covering all the basics from the architecture of its system on a chip (SoC) to running a full OS and finally running code that interfaces with electrical circuits attached to its GPIO pins. That's a lot to go over, and we've only scratched the surface. Now it's time to take what we've learned and apply it to projects that will take the Tinker Board to the next level as a practical tool. The first project that we're going to look at has become an increasingly popular project among single-board computer users: a game emulation system.

What Is Emulation?

Game emulation is a software-based process that emulates the hardware characteristics of gaming systems or computer architectures. This allows your computer or other device to run games or other programs that would otherwise be incompatible. Single-board computers are great choices for emulator hardware because of their form factor, system specs, and ability to run Linux. This makes the Tinker Board and Tinker Board S especially appealing as emulation hardware with their higher-than-average SoC specs.

© Liz Clark 2019
L. Clark, *Practical Tinker Board*, https://doi.org/10.1007/978-1-4842-3826-4_7

Even though game emulation is often targeted at hardware that is much older and underpowered compared to modern hardware, system specs do matter. You may think that if you're trying to emulate a system that had utilized an 8-bit architecture you don't have to worry about the speed of your CPU or amount of RAM, but because everything is software-based, system specs become a paramount concern and the higher the spec the better. An underpowered system can ruin an emulation experience and render the emulator and emulated program unusable.

There are many ways to emulate games, and often your final choice will come down to preference. For this project we're going to look at a specialized Linux distribution option for gaming emulation called Lakka. We'll walk through how to set up and navigate Lakka for the Tinker Board.

ROMs

Before we go any further, though, we need to address the elephant that always sneaks into the room during any discussion on game emulation: the legality of ROMs. ROM stands for read-only memory and is a reference to the chips found on old game cartridges that held the game data that would be read by the gaming system. Despite its hardware origin, the term *ROM* has come to be used for the digital files of these old games and programs.

There is a lot of debate and discussion surrounding the use of ROMs for off-the-shelf games that would have been purchased in cartridge form back in the day. Is their very existence legal, let alone their active use inside emulation software? These legal considerations vary based on your location and the original game publisher's specifications for each game, so be sure to do your research.

There are games and other programs available that do not carry these considerations, though, such as games that exist in the public domain, open source projects, and games made by independent developers, often called homebrew games.

Lakka

The emulation OS that we're going to use here is Lakka. As previously stated, Lakka is a specialized Linux distribution for retro gaming emulation. It's a fork of another Linux distro called LibreELEC that we'll also look at in the next chapter.

Lakka is built on top of RetroArch, which is an open source project for a front-end API that many emulators are based on. RetroArch has been ported to run on many platforms as a standalone program, from modern game consoles to desktop Windows computers. As a front-end, RetroArch controls the GUI, controller inputs, video settings, and similar settings for the emulators.

The actual emulation process takes place on the back end with what are called cores that are built with Libretro, an additional open source project that is built in tandem with RetroArch. Each core is a different game system or older hardware emulator that can be loaded into RetroArch to run corresponding ROMs. The cores take care of the processing and running the code behind the scenes, making Libretro and RetroArch a great pairing of software.

Lakka's purpose in all of this is basically to load RetroArch upon boot. Instead of implementing the traditional Linux desktop or other GUI, Lakka has only the basics necessary to boot up and load RetroArch automatically. As a result, no other software can really be loaded onto Lakka. Its sole purpose is to run RetroArch. With this setup you are setting yourself up for the best possible emulation experience, since your hardware will not be tied up with any additional back-end processes aside from running the emulators.

Downloading and Installing Lakka

To download the Lakka disk image, we need to navigate to its main builds page at le.builds.lakka.tv, which is separate from the main Lakka web site. This page has every single build available for a multitude of different hardware, some of which would be considered beta or even alpha builds. As of the writing of this chapter, Lakka is not considered to be 100% stable for full release for the Tinker Board, which is why the Tinker Board's build is located on this page.

Once you've navigated to le.builds.lakka.tv, scroll down the page to the Rockchip.Tinkerboard.arm/ link, as shown in Figure 7-1.

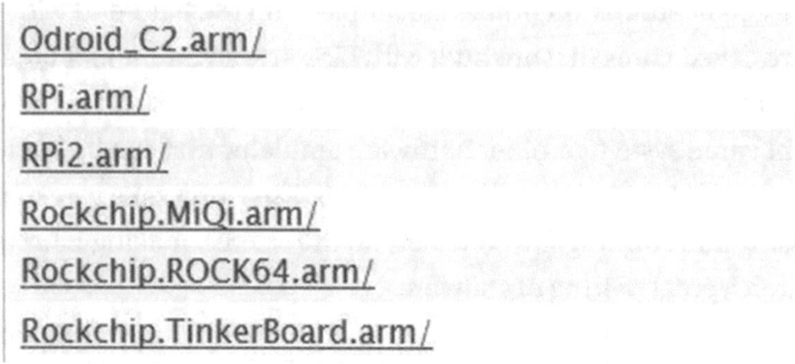

Odroid_C2.arm/
RPi.arm/
RPi2.arm/
Rockchip.MiQi.arm/
Rockchip.ROCK64.arm/
Rockchip.TinkerBoard.arm/

Figure 7-1. *The link to the Lakka builds for the Tinker Board*

Click that link to access the different image files available for the Tinker Board. We want to use the most recent release with the img.gz file extension, which at the time of writing is the 2.1 release dated 22-Nov-2017 12:38 as shown in Figure 7-2. Click on that disk image to begin downloading.

Index of /Rockchip.TinkerBoard.arm/

File Name ↓	File Size ↓	Date ↓
Parent directory/	-	-
Lakka-Rockchip.TinkerBoard.arm-2.1-rc5.img.gz	268M	11-Oct-2017 07:26
Lakka-Rockchip.TinkerBoard.arm-2.1-rc5.img.gz.md5	87	11-Oct-2017 07:24
Lakka-Rockchip.TinkerBoard.arm-2.1-rc5.img.gz.s...>	119	11-Oct-2017 07:24
Lakka-Rockchip.TinkerBoard.arm-2.1-rc5.tar	289M	11-Oct-2017 07:25
Lakka-Rockchip.TinkerBoard.arm-2.1-rc5.tar.md5	84	11-Oct-2017 07:24
Lakka-Rockchip.TinkerBoard.arm-2.1-rc5.tar.sha256	116	11-Oct-2017 07:24
Lakka-Rockchip.TinkerBoard.arm-2.1-rc6.img.gz	276M	10-Nov-2017 14:29
Lakka-Rockchip.TinkerBoard.arm-2.1-rc6.img.gz.md5	87	10-Nov-2017 14:29
Lakka-Rockchip.TinkerBoard.arm-2.1-rc6.img.gz.s...>	119	10-Nov-2017 14:28
Lakka-Rockchip.TinkerBoard.arm-2.1-rc6.tar	298M	10-Nov-2017 14:29
Lakka-Rockchip.TinkerBoard.arm-2.1-rc6.tar.md5	84	10-Nov-2017 14:28
Lakka-Rockchip.TinkerBoard.arm-2.1-rc6.tar.sha256	116	10-Nov-2017 14:28
Lakka-Rockchip.TinkerBoard.arm-2.1.img.gz	271M	22-Nov-2017 12:38
Lakka-Rockchip.TinkerBoard.arm-2.1.img.gz.md5	83	22-Nov-2017 12:38
Lakka-Rockchip.TinkerBoard.arm-2.1.img.gz.sha256	115	22-Nov-2017 12:38
Lakka-Rockchip.TinkerBoard.arm-2.1.tar	293M	22-Nov-2017 12:38
Lakka-Rockchip.TinkerBoard.arm-2.1.tar.md5	80	22-Nov-2017 12:38
Lakka-Rockchip.TinkerBoard.arm-2.1.tar.sha256	112	22-Nov-2017 12:38

Figure 7-2. *A list of the available Lakka disk images for the Tinker Board. Notice the version numbers, file extensions, and dates.*

Next reformat your microSD card or the eMMC flash module on the Tinker Board S, following the directions in Chapter 3. As with any operating system install, it's important to start with fresh media for best results.

Note   It's recommended to use a storage device with a capacity of at least 16GB and a speed of at least 10Mbps. Otherwise, you may run into compatibility issues.

After a fresh reformat, open Etcher, the program we used in Chapter 3 to burn the TinkerOS and Android disk images. Select the newly downloaded Lakka disk image in Etcher and choose your microSD card or eMMC flash on the Tinker Board S as the targeted disk, and then flash the Lakka image, as shown in Figure 7-3.

Figure 7-3. *The Lakka disk image loaded into Etcher*

First Boot

After flashing the Lakka image to your selected storage device, you can
power up the Tinker Board for the first boot. Much as it does with other
operating systems, the first boot takes a bit longer than subsequent boots.
During Lakka's first boot, the file system will be resized and then finally
boot into the landing page for RetroArch.

Here will be a test of whether your chosen storage is too small or too
slow. If Lakka seems to get stuck at all, that is probably the case. Again, it's
recommended to use a storage device that is at least 16GB and has speeds
comparable to SDHC cards.

The landing page for RetroArch on Lakka has a light blue background
with a swirling wave animation by default. Since Lakka is a gaming OS,
you have a few choices for GUI navigation. You can stick with a keyboard
and use the arrows, Enter, and backspace keys for navigation, or you can
use a gamepad. This can be connected via either USB or Bluetooth (after
you enable Bluetooth within Lakka, which we will go over shortly). For
navigation, there are tile icons at the top of the GUI for different setting

categories. From left to right by default are the Main Menu, Settings, Favorites, History, Netplay Rooms and Import Content, as shown in Figure 7-4.

Figure 7-4. *The Lakka GUI*

Navigating Lakka: the Main Menu

The Main Menu category allows you to quickly adjust the main functions in RetroArch. The Load Core menu lists all the cores available by default in Lakka, as shown in Figure 7-5. You can select different cores to use for different system emulations or check here if you upload a core that is not included by default.

Figure 7-5. *The Load Core menu. All of these cores are built with libretro.*

Load Content allows you to load ROMs, media, and other files that you've added into Lakka's file system. The Online Updater lets you update Lakka in case there is a new build available, making it basically a GUI version of sudo apt-get update and upgrade. The Thumbnails Updater has options to update the thumbnails for ROMs, and finally the Content Downloader offers other emulation engines and add-ons that are available and compatible with Lakka but for various reasons, such as storage space concerns or niche popularity, are not included by default in Lakka. You can choose any of these from the list to download and install, as shown in Figure 7-6.

Figure 7-6. *The Content Downloader menu*

Note   In order for any options to appear in the Content Downloader menu, you need to have the Tinker Board connected to the Internet.

The Information tab has information available for the network, the system, databases, and search history. The Network Information basically houses your IP address, which we'll be referencing shortly in this chapter. System Information shows information about the Lakka build version that you're running and your system specs, as shown in Figure 7-7. The Database Manager shows the different emulation databases installed, and the Cursor Manager shows the system's search history.

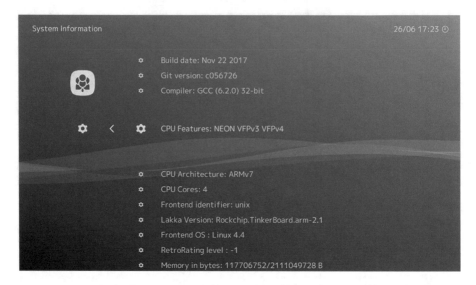

Figure 7-7. *The System Information for the Tinker Board in Lakka.*
Some of these specs will look quite familiar now.

The last three options on the Main menu are utilities for Lakka. Quit
RetroArch exits the program (and then goes right back into it since there
is nothing else to run on Lakka besides RetroArch), Reboot reboots the
system, and Shutdown safely shuts everything down.

Settings

The Settings menu offers more detailed options for Lakka, such as Video,
Audio and Interface settings. Under Video, you can fine-tune how your
ROMs will run. This can be especially important with older games from
the 1980s and early 90s that were meant to be played on CRT monitors,
which displayed and processed video signals much differently than today's
LCD monitors. The games were often programmed to work with the CRT
technologies, and this often translates poorly to modern displays. There are
ways around this in software, though, and the cores take care of a lot of it;
but retro gaming aficionados will have preferences that can be adjusted here,
such as V-Sync, Integer Scale, and Aspect Ratio as shown in Figure 7-8.

Figure 7-8. *The Video Settings page*

Audio settings allow you to mute or unmute audio, adjust the overall volume level, and choose your audio device. Input allows you to set up hotkeys for your chosen controller, and the User Interface has editable options for Lakka's appearance. You can edit which items are available on the menu screen, set up kiosk mode, and customize the appearance of Lakka. Kiosk mode lets you run Lakka so that no one can edit the settings. This can be handy for setups where your device is going to be publicly available. For the Appearance options, you can set up a custom background image, change the icon theme, adjust the color theme, and change thumbnail options for ROMs as shown in Figure 7-9.

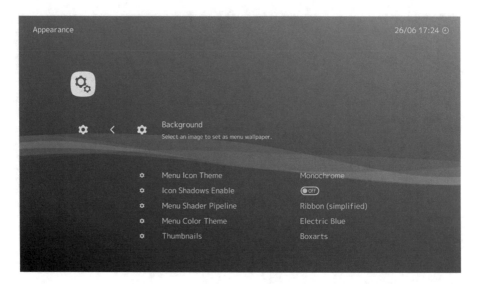

Figure 7-9. *Editable Appearance options for Lakka. Much like other operating systems we've looked at, the GUI has a lot of customization options.*

Wi-Fi lets you connect to a wireless network. Simply select it from the menu, and Lakka will scan for available networks. Once yours appears, select it and enter your password. You'll now be connected to Wi-Fi. You won't need to be connected to the Internet to successfully use Lakka, but it can be useful for some tasks.

The Services tab allows you to toggle on and off SSH, Samba, and Bluetooth, as shown in Figure 7-10. SSH provides remote access to the command line. Since Lakka does not have an easily accessible terminal, this can be very handy. You'll just need an SSH client on another computer to connect to the Tinker Board. Samba is open source software that enables file sharing across different platforms over a network. This means that Windows, Apple, and Linux systems can all share files with a lot of back-end work. By enabling Samba in Lakka, you can share files between your Lakka build on the Tinker Board and your main system. The final service is Bluetooth, which allows you to connect Bluetooth devices, in particular Bluetooth controllers.

Figure 7-10. *The Services menu. All three Services can be toggled on or off*

Favorites, History, Netplay, and Import Content

Moving on to the last few menus, Favorites will eventually populate with ROMs that you mark as favorites and add to playlists as mentioned earlier. History will also populate after you play a few games, showing the most recently played in a list. Netplay is a feature of RetroArch that allows you to play multiplayer games between two different builds of Lakka. Import Content is the utility used to import any media, including ROMs, into your Lakka install. We'll go over how to do this shortly.

Importing ROMs into Lakka

Now that we've toured Lakka's GUI, we can start using it properly by first loading in some ROMs. There are a few methods for loading ROMs and other content into Lakka. We'll go over two methods that are OS-agnostic, meaning that no matter which desktop operating system you're using, whether Windows, macOS, or Linux, you'll be able to follow these steps to load ROMs onto Lakka on the Tinker Board.

Loading ROMs over the Network

The first method we'll discuss is loading ROMs over the network from your computer to the Tinker Board. To do this, both devices need to be on the same network, either wirelessly or wired. For Lakka, make sure you either enable and connect to Wi-Fi as discussed earlier in the chapter or connect an Ethernet cable to the Tinker Board.

Once the Tinker Board is online, go to your computer and open your file browser. Enter your Tinker Board's IP address, which can be found under Main Menu ➤ Information ➤ Network Information in Lakka, at the top of your file directory's window using the proper IP syntax for your operating system.

After connecting to the Tinker Board's IP address, you'll see Lakka's file system as shown in Figure 7-11. You'll be able to add, remove, or edit any of the files within Lakka using this method, but for now we're going to stick with adding ROMs.

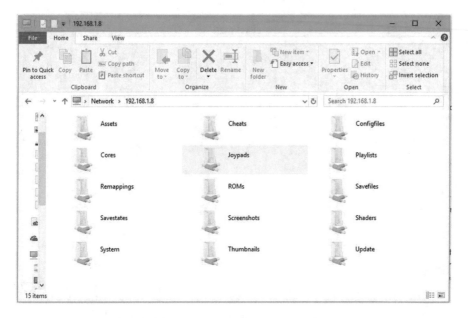

Figure 7-11. *Lakka's file system viewed remotely*

You've probably figured out by looking at Figure 7-11 that ROMs are stored in the ROMs folder in Lakka. Open that folder and then open a second file directory window on your computer to navigate to your locally stored ROMs that you want to transfer to the Tinker Board.

Next, inside Lakka's ROMs folder, create a new folder for each system that your soon-to-be-transferred ROMs will run on, as shown in Figure 7-12.

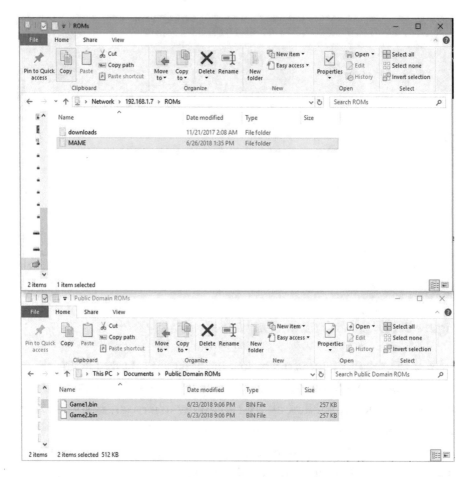

Figure 7-12. *A new folder has been created in Lakka's ROMs folder, and your locally stored ROMs are queued up*

For example, if you have ROMs for NES, create an NES folder and if you have ROMs for MAME, create a MAME folder. After creating that folder, open it and then drag and drop your locally stored ROMs to their destination folders on Lakka. You should see them appear in the folders as shown in Figure 7-13.

Figure 7-13. *Locally stored ROMs successfully copied to Lakka's
ROMs folder*

Moving back to the Tinker Board, navigate to the Import Content header
and select Scan Directory from the drop-down. After scanning, you'll see the
folders for the different systems that were created. Enter one of the folders
and then select <Scan This Directory> as shown in Figure 7-14.

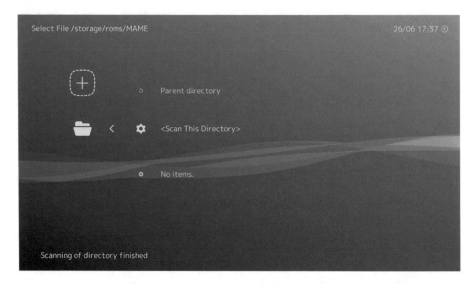

Figure 7-14. *The directory scan function for Lakka's local ROMs folder*

Messages will flash at the bottom of the screen that the directory is being scanned and then that the scanning is complete. Nothing else will show-up here to let you know that the ROMs were loaded successfully. To verify this, navigate to the Main Menu and then select Load Content. Under Load Content, select Collections, which is where the scanned items will appear. After entering Collections, you should see your newly scanned folder available. Enter that folder and you'll see your ROMs, as shown in Figure 7-15.

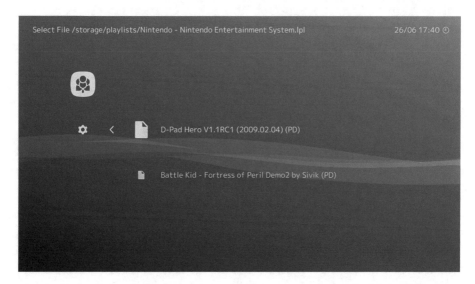

Figure 7-15. *A list of ROMs added via the network. Both of these games are homebrewed by independent developers and as a result are a part of the public domain.*

Loading ROMs over USB

If you have an exceedingly large ROM collection or you don't want to connect your Lakka system to your network, you also have the option to load ROMs from a USB drive. To do this we first need to format the USB drive to a compatible format for Lakka. The preferred formats are FAT, NTFS, and exFat.

After formatting, simply copy your ROM files to the USB drive and connect it to the Tinker Board. You can now either scan the USB drive's directory or search for individual ROM files on the USB drive. The drive will show-up as a folder in the directory listings, as seen in Figure 7-16.

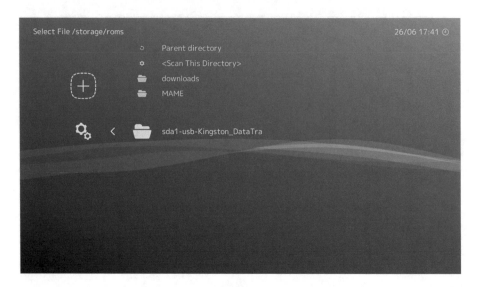

Figure 7-16. *The USB drive mounted in Lakka*

After scanning, your ROMs will appear in the Collections folder under Load Content, just as the ROMs previously imported via network did after scanning. If you don't want to add a ROM permanently to your collection, you can also access the ROM by going to the Start Directory folder under Load Content. The USB drive will appear as a folder there, as shown in Figure 7-17, and ROMs will be selectable for play.

Figure 7-17. *The USB drive is also accessible under the Main Menu*

Playing Games

To play a ROM, select it from Collections, Favorites, or other preferred location in Lakka. After selecting it, you'll be greeted with a menu with the options Run, Add to Favorites, and Information, as shown in Figure 7-18.

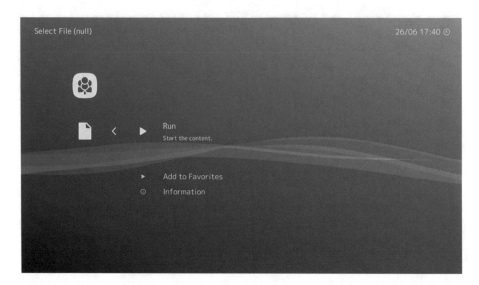

Figure 7-18. *The ROM menu*

If your ROM collection is large, you may want to create a Favorites list where you can easily access frequently played games. Information lists the full file name of the ROM, and Run starts the game. Once inside the game, you'll use your preferred controller to play just as you would if playing on the original hardware.

Once a game is running, the Quick Menu will appear under the Main Menu. In the Quick Menu, you can access save states and other in-game settings that are unique to Lakka. This allows you to save your progress in games created for systems that wouldn't traditionally allow save states or load ROMs from these save states. This menu is only available when a ROM is running in the background. Once the ROM is exited or the system is rebooted, the Quick Menu will disappear.

Connecting via SSH

Even though Lakka has a detailed GUI that lets you access almost every setting, you may find yourself missing the command line. Although accessing the terminal is not possible on single-board computer builds of Lakka at this time, you can access it remotely from a desktop computer.

First enable SSH under Settings ➤ Services on Lakka. After that, move to your desktop system. If you're using macOS or Linux, you can simply open a terminal to log in via SSH. Once you open a terminal, type in ssh root@ followed by the IP of the Tinker Board with no spaces. For example, if your IP was 111.111.1.1 you would type ssh root@111.111.1.1 and then hit enter to connect. You'll then be prompted for a password, which is root.

SSH is not a built-in feature on Windows. As a result, you'll need a third-party SSH client. A popular and simple one to use is called PuTTY.[1] After downloading and installing PuTTY, select SSH and enter Lakka's IP address as shown in Figure 7-19.

---

[1]More information on PuTTY, including a link to download, can be found on PuTTY's web site: https://www.putty.org/

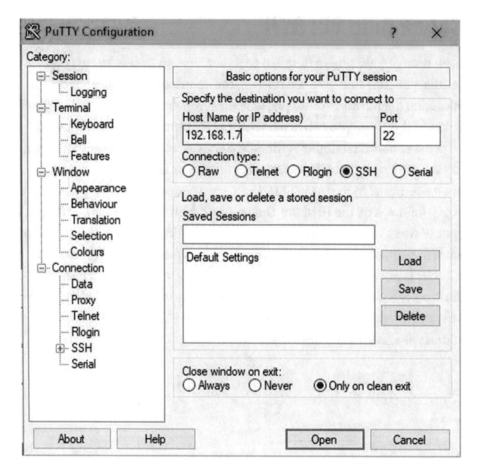

Figure 7-19. *PuTTY's GUI window. Notice that SSH is selected as the connection type. Also note that your IP address will be different.*

Click Open to initiate the connection, which will open a terminal window. You'll be asked for the username, which is root, followed by the password, which is also root. After that, a message will appear in the terminal showing that you've successfully connected, as in Figure 7-20.

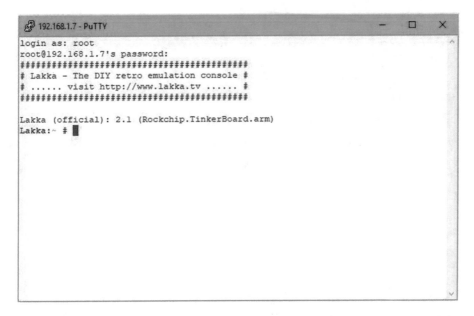

Figure 7-20. *A successful login to the Tinker Board running Lakka via SSH*

Once you're connected you can use any Linux terminal command. A useful scenario would be to use ls to see a list of file directories, as shown in Figure 7-21.

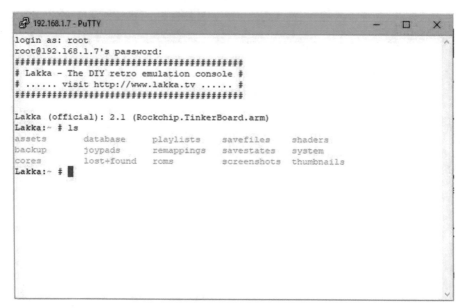

Figure 7-21. *The results of the* ls *command*

You can also use cd to change directories and view, for example, the file directory for the ROMs folder, as shown in Figure 7-22.

Figure 7-22. *The results of the* ls *command in the ROMs folder*

There is no need to use sudo when accessing the command line in Lakka, as it's a LibreELEC build of Linux and does not require that clearance. If you do use sudo, you'll get an error message like the one in Figure 7-23. You can reboot and shut down via the terminal as well, just as with other Linux distros, as also shown in Figure 7-23.

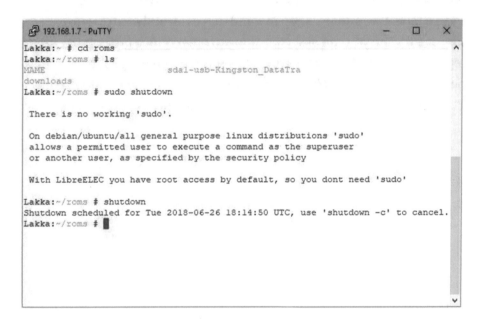

Figure 7-23. *The sudo command is not necessary when using the terminal with Lakka*

Note   If you shut down the Tinker Board or exit the terminal window, you'll close your SSH connection to the Tinker Board and will have to reconnect.

Wrapping Things Up

Using your Tinker Board as an emulation system is a fun and simple project that goes beyond the basic desktop tasks that we've looked at in previous chapters. The developers of Lakka have done a great job in porting over a build for the Tinker Board, which is a testament to the open source community. Keep in mind that as an end user of open source software you can also contribute to open source projects by simply reporting bugs to developers and with some experience testing pre-release builds. For now, let's look at some more specialized Linux distros for the Tinker Board to build additional projects in the upcoming chapters.

## CHAPTER 8

Project 2: Use the Tinker Board as a Media Center with Kodi

One of the Tinker Board's most enticing features is its ability to play back 4K video. That combined with its SoC specs makes it a great candidate to act as a media player. Much as in our last project, where we set up the Tinker Board to be a dedicated game emulation system, we're now going to try setting it up with Kodi, a popular open source media center application.

LibreELEC

We're going to set up Kodi by using LibreELEC as the OS. LibreELEC is a lightweight Linux distribution that has the motto "just enough OS," which is often shorthanded to JeOS. It's open source, and it's encouraged for the community to develop their own builds for niche or newer hardware that becomes available. LibreELEC also does extensive testing for its official releases and strives to keep everything bug-free.

© Liz Clark 2019
L. Clark, *Practical Tinker Board*, https://doi.org/10.1007/978-1-4842-3826-4_8

Upon booting, LibreELEC boots directly to Kodi just like the way Lakka boots directly into RetroArch. Coincidentally, as mentioned briefly in the last chapter, Lakka is a fork of LibreELEC and as a result they both share a lot of the same architecture.

What Is Kodi?

The main star of the show is Kodi, with LibreELEC basically acting as a way to get Kodi to launch. As previously mentioned, Kodi is also open source and is media center software with a lot of options and customizability. Its focus is video and audio playback from files that are stored locally, either on the main OS disk or attached storage, or files that are available via a shared network drive. Kodi can access these network drives, whether they are independent NAS setups or a shared portion of a computer's hard drive, to stream for playback.

This chapter isn't going to be a walkthrough for using Kodi per se, since it has so many features available. This chapter is more to show you how to set up Kodi on the Tinker Board so that you can then use those tools to customize your installation of Kodi with LibreELEC to fit your preferences and needs. Just as with RetroArch, the use of many of Kodi's features depends on user preference and use case scenario.

Legal Considerations for Kodi

Just as we've had to address legal concerns surrounding copyright with previous entries in this book, there are some things to touch on with Kodi. In the form that is built and distributed by the development team, Team Kodi, and the XMBC Foundation, Kodi is completely legal and free from piracy. This is the same version that is distributed in LibreELEC.

Third-party independent developers will sometimes create add-ons for Kodi that enable piracy or illegal torrenting, similar to issues with Android APKs online. This doesn't mean that Kodi is bad, since it is not a problem unique to Kodi. The same types of software are constantly being built for basically every piece of software and operating system that allows an Internet connection. Team Kodi and the XMBC Foundation both denounce these illicit add-ons.

Basically, if you stick to accessing your own personal media library that you've obtained legally, then you are using Kodi for its intended purpose: to make personal media consumption and library organization hassle-free and convenient. With this public service announcement out of the way, let's jump into some more background on LibreELEC for the Tinker Board and begin the setup process.

LibreELEC for the Tinker Board

As we discussed previously when introducing LibreELEC, its developers encourage community builds for different pieces of hardware that may not be initially supported in the official build. As of writing this book, the Tinker Board is one of those boards that benefited from a community build and is now seeing an official build in development. You can check the progress of the build and file bugs and pull requests via the project page that is a branch of the full LibreELEC build on GitHub.[1]

As you can see in Figure 8-1, which is a project feature checklist, not everything is supported yet that you would expect to find in Kodi, but a lot is currently supported, and we have a more than viable media player, including popular video and audio file playback support.

---

[1]The Tinker Board branch of the LibreELEC project can be found on GitHub here: `https://github.com/LibreELEC/LibreELEC.tv/tree/master/projects/Rockchip/devices/TinkerBoard`

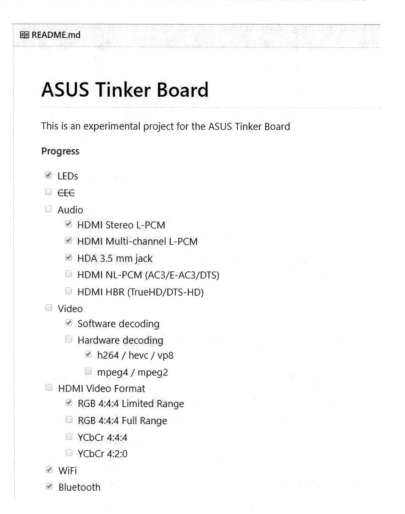

Figure 8-1. *The project features checklist on GitHub for the Tinker Board*

CEC

One notable item not in the checklist is CEC (consumer electronics control). This feature, in the form of a serial bus, along with HDMI allows you to control multiple devices with the same remote control. If you've ever had a remote for your television that can also control functions with a DVD player or cable box that was connected via HDMI, then you were using CEC.

There is a note on the GitHub repo's feature checklist for the LibreELEC Tinker Board port under "Known Issues/Limitations" that CEC is not connected to the SoC, and as a result is unusable, as shown in Figure 8-2.

Known Issues/Limitations

- Video output is RGB 4:4:4 8-bit limited range
- Video aspect ratio / zoom is not working for all modes
- Generic USB-Audio do not work due to a custom alsa config
- 4K resolution is limited to 30hz due to failed compliance test
- CEC is not connected to SoC

Figure 8-2. *The Known Issues/Limitations in the project features checklist on GitHub for the Tinker Board. Notice specifically the note on CEC not being connected to the SoC.*

This is true for the original Tinker Board. In fact, there was a post on the Tinker Board forum by a user who investigated whether CEC would be functional and discovered that it was not hooked up by tracing the signal on the board.[2] For the Tinker Board S, however, CEC is connected and ready to use. If this feature is of interest to you, especially for something like Kodi, then the Tinker Board S is a better option than the original Tinker Board in this scenario.

LibreELEC ISO for the Tinker Board

You may have noticed in perusing the repo that there isn't an ISO available for download; it's all source files. This is on purpose. Since the community builds are not official releases from LibreELEC, often the developers working on side builds are posting their work as a proof of concept or for

---

[2]The forum post with pictures on tracing the CEC connection on the original Tinker Board: `https://tinkerboarding.co.uk/forum/archive/index.php/thread-258.html`

other developers to view and contribute with the intention that anyone interested at that time would compile their own build, or ISO, to test on the hardware. So how are we going to use LibreELEC?

So far in this book we've downloaded precompiled disk images to burn onto our preferred boot media for the Tinker Board. Before we downloaded those images, someone had to compile them or build from source code. For this LibreELEC build, you're going to be that person. If you've never done this before, it may seem intimidating. But after everything we've done in this book so far with the terminal and Linux, you should be just fine running your own cross-compilation.

Note   If you are truly uncomfortable following the cross-compilation steps, you can find a hosted ISO for the LibreELEC build for the Tinker Board on a LibreELEC test image site, similar to the web site we used for Lakka.[3] There will also be a link to an ISO on the GitHub repo associated with this book that was compiled following these instructions, but for best results, and a guarantee of being up to date, it's recommended to perform an independent cross-compile. It will also be beneficial for your continuing Linux education and future Tinker Board projects. Eventually, as development continues, an official LibreELEC release image may become available for the Tinker Board.

What Is Cross-compiling?

Before we hop on a terminal we need to go over some basics. Cross-compilation is the process of compiling code for one platform on a different platform. For example, if you compiled an Android ISO on a PC running Windows 10, that would be considered a cross-compilation.

---

[3]The LibreELEC test image web site, posted and hosted by LibreELEC developers: http://kwiboo.libreelec.tv/test/

This is quite common for developers to do since it's convenient to compile where you do all your work, and a developer's workstation probably has more power than the platform they're developing for.

That is one consideration for compilation in general: it can be a slow process, especially for operating system ISOs. With a modern hardware setup, assuming a multi-core CPU, a minimum 8GB of RAM, and of course a solid-state hard drive, you can expect it to take at least two to three hours for this version of LibreELEC. Extreme cases can take more than eight hours. So do not expect to be launching Etcher with your newly compiled ISO immediately after launching the process from the terminal. That shouldn't dissuade you from doing this, though; it's just the nature of the process.

Ubuntu

Since this process for LibreELEC takes place in Linux, we're going to need access to a Linux operating system to cross-compile. There are a few options for this, but for this tutorial, we're going to use Ubuntu, a very popular desktop Linux distribution that many people use as their daily operating system. After using TinkerOS you're guaranteed to be able to navigate Ubuntu comfortably.

There are a few options for how to run Ubuntu. You can run it from a bootable USB drive on your main computer. This is a very popular option for people who have only one computer and do not want to commit to using Ubuntu full time. The installation process allows Ubuntu to be run live from the USB without affecting your main system. Normally, it doesn't matter too much what size USB drive you use for a live Ubuntu installation, but for cross-compiling you will want to use one that is at least 64GB in size.

You can also set up a virtual machine (VM) for those who utilize virtualization. Much as with the USB size consideration, you will want to make sure that you allocate enough processes for it. You can also, of course, run a full install of Ubuntu on a computer to have a dedicated Linux system. You can do this by buying or building a computer from scratch for this purpose or by installing Ubuntu onto an internal hard drive and then attaching it to your computer's motherboard. It is recommended to detach your main system's hard drives while utilizing this approach to avoid any storage issues. This is also only suggested for people who have experience with desktop computer hardware.

Finally, you could also run Ubuntu on a single-board computer. There are many builds available for different platforms. This avoids touching or affecting your main computer in any way; however, the cross compilation process will definitely be slower than the other options, and storage space could also be a concern in this configuration. There is also a chance that the SoC's architecture could cause unexpected incompatibilities at points during the compilation and cause a failure.

Bootable USB for Ubuntu

For the purposes of this chapter, we're going to use the bootable USB option for Ubuntu since it offers minimum risk to your hardware while also having a high chance of a successful compilation. We will go over the basics of creating a bootable USB for Ubuntu, but it is recommended to follow along directly with the resources provided by Canonical, the maintainers of Ubuntu, on the official Ubuntu web site (`https://www.ubuntu.com`) in case there are any changes.

The first step, no matter which operating system you're working on, is to format your USB drive. You'll want to format the drive as FAT or FAT32. After that, you'll download the Ubuntu ISO from Ubuntu and using a disk imaging tool, either Etcher, Rufus, or a built-in program, you'll write the ISO to your USB drive, the same way we've imaged all the operating systems so far for the Tinker Board.

After the USB is all set, you'll reboot your computer and navigate to either the BIOS, for Windows and Linux, or the bootpicker, for macOS, to choose to boot into Ubuntu on the USB drive. Traditionally in Windows and Linux you'll hold down F12 to access this. For macOS, hold down ALT to access the bootpicker.

Run the Cross-Compilation

After you finish setting up Ubuntu and feel comfortable with the GUI, we can get started with the cross-compilation process. We'll be following the cross-compile instructions from LibreELEC.[4] Check to make sure you have an Internet connection and then navigate to the terminal in Ubuntu. If you haven't already, run sudo apt-get update followed by sudo apt-get upgrade. Then, to be on the safe side, reboot Ubuntu using sudo reboot.

After that, install the dependencies for the cross-compile by running sudo apt install gcc make git unzip wget xz-utils. Many of these come preconfigured on Ubuntu, but it's always good to double-check. Next, we're going to clone the GitHub repository for LibeELEC, just as we cloned the C and Python GPIO libraries in TinkerOS for the GPIO chapter. To do this, we're going to run git clone https://github.com/LibreELEC/LibreELEC.tv.git.

Next, we're going to move into the LibreELEC.tv folder by running cd ~/LibreELEC.tv. If you cloned the repo into a different folder than the Home folder, then you'll of course have to change into that directory.

The next and final step is to initiate the cross-compilation. Again, this will take a minimum of two to three hours, so be sure that you're ready to commit to the process before starting. The cross-compile for LibreELEC is based in a make file. The make file requires that you select the project, device (if named), and architecture that you're building for. If you refer to the Tinker Board's LibreELEC repo page, at the bottom these specifications are listed for the Tinker Board, PROJECT=Rockchip DEVICE=TinkerBoard ARCH=arm, as shown in Figure 8-3. Notice that PROJECT, DEVICE, and ARCHITECTURE must appear in all caps, and there are no spaces between the equal sign and the named parameters. This is all very important to the make file's syntax.

---

[4]https://wiki.libreelec.tv/compile

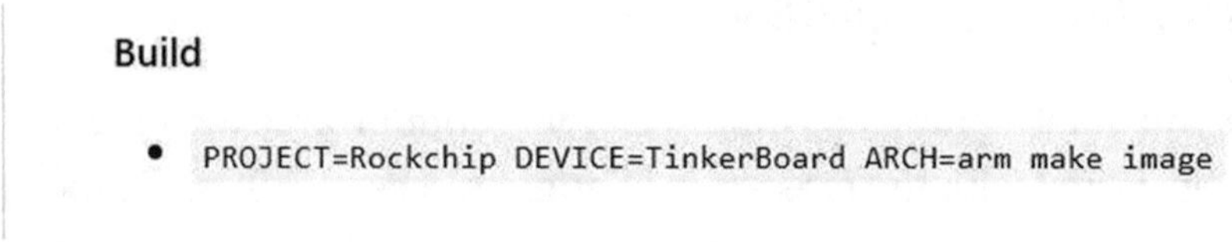

Build

- `PROJECT=Rockchip DEVICE=TinkerBoard ARCH=arm make image`

Figure 8-3. *The build syntax specifications for the Tinker Board as listed on GitHub*

Once you're sure you're ready to begin the cross compile, enter

```
PROJECT=Rockchip DEVICE=TinkerBoard ARCH=arm make image
```

into the terminal, and the process will begin. The terminal will have text scrolling by extremely fast and will also seem to suddenly pause and start-up again. This is all normal while all the scripts in the make file run. Do not exit the terminal window, and to be on the safe side don't try to run any other tasks while the cross-compile is running. It's best to let all the computer's resources be dedicated to the build.

Note   If you want to know more about LibreELEC's compilation process, see their wiki entry on the topic here: `https://wiki.libreelec.tv/compile`.

Burn the ISO

After the cross-compile finishes, navigate to the LibreELEC.tv folder via Ubuntu's GUI. Locate the target folder and open it. There you'll see the ISO file in an img.gz format. You'll notice that there are a few other file types in the folder, as shown in Figure 8-4.

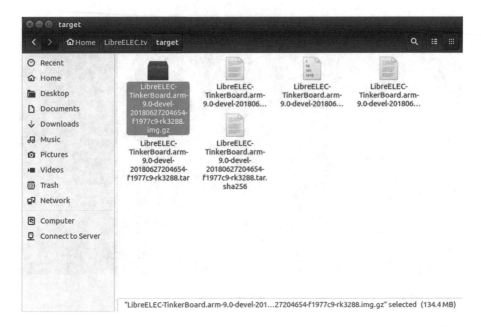

Figure 8-4. *The compiled files for LibreELEC for the Tinker Board*

If you remember the downloads available for Lakka (Figure 7-2 in Chapter 7) for the Tinker Board, you'll notice that your freshly compiled LibreELEC files are identical file types. This is again related to the fact that Lakka is a fork of LibreELEC.

To make things simple, you can burn the ISO directly in Ubuntu to either an SD card or the eMMC on the Tinker Board S. Download Etcher from etcher.io and then launch the program. As discussed in Chapter 3, the GUI is identical in Etcher across platforms. Then, load the img.gz file, select your media, and then burn the ISO. After Etcher finishes, you're ready to boot into LibreELEC on the Tinker Board.

First Boot

During the first boot of LibreELEC, you'll be brought through a setup wizard that will help you get started, as shown in Figure 8-5.

Figure 8-5. *The LibreELEC setup wizard*

In the first step, you'll be asked if you want to change the hostname to reflect where the device is located. This is helpful if you have multiple devices running LibreELEC, since the default hostname is simply "LibreELEC." For this chapter, we're going to leave the default hostname.

Next, you'll be prompted to connect to a Wi-Fi network. A list of available networks will appear at the bottom of the window. Select your network and enter your password to connect. After that, you'll have the opportunity to turn SSH and Samba services on. If you don't turn them on now, don't worry—we'll be going over all these important settings shortly; including SSH and Samba.

Finally, to close out the wizard, the final window acts as a thank you from LibreELEC for choosing to run LibreELEC. It also lists some information on the LibreELEC project that we also discussed at the beginning of this chapter.

After going through the initial setup, you'll see the default GUI layout, as shown in Figure 8-6.

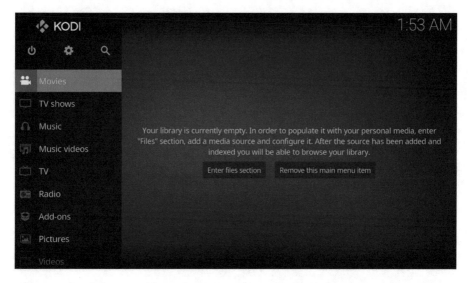

Figure 8-6.   *The Kodi landing page GUI. Notice the different media types on the left.*

On the left, there are media categories, such as Movies, Music, TV Shows, and so on. In the top-right corner, you'll see a clock, and in the top-left corner below the Kodi logo you'll see icons for Power, Settings, and Search. The Power icon allows you to shut down the system, shut down the system with a delay by setting up a timer, and reboot the system, as shown in Figure 8-7. The Shutdown with delay option allows you to enter in the delay in the form of minutes, similar to shutdown timers you may have seen on televisions.

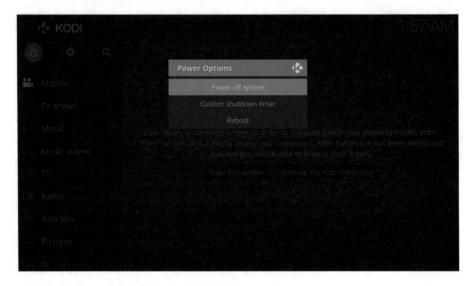

Figure 8-7. *Kodi's power options*

System Settings

The cog wheel icon brings you to the System settings page, as shown in Figure 8-8. On this page you can access a variety of settings to fully configure and set up Kodi. We're going to look at a few important settings that we'll be referencing throughout the chapter.

Figure 8-8. *The System settings. Notice the different categories.*

System Info

First let's look at System Info, which will display everything you need to know about your Tinker Board while it's running Kodi. The Summary page shows how much memory you have available, the IP address (which we'll need shortly), the screen resolution, and system uptime. At the bottom of the screen for all the categories in System info you'll also see a live status bar showing system CPU usage and system memory usage, as shown in Figure 8-9.

Figure 8-9. *The live status bar in System Info for CPU and memory usage*

Storage shows you the storage devices currently connected to the Tinker Board and their index address. Network shows you more detailed network information, including the MAC address. Video shows information on the GPU and OpenGL version. Finally, Hardware shows information on the CPU along with the current temperature of the CPU.

One important note about LibreELEC currently for the Tinker Board is that it causes the Tinker Board to run a bit hot, with an average temperature of 150° to 160°F or 65° to 71°C with the stock heatsink installed. If you're planning to run this long-term, especially in an enclosed area, you may want to consider adding a fan or larger heat sink to the Tinker Board's cooling solution.

System

The System category holds settings for video, audio, controllers, and other similar options. Under Display, you can change the resolution and refresh rate, as shown in Figure 8-10. The Tinker Board can push 4K/30 comfortably, but anything above that is not guaranteed to play back smoothly.

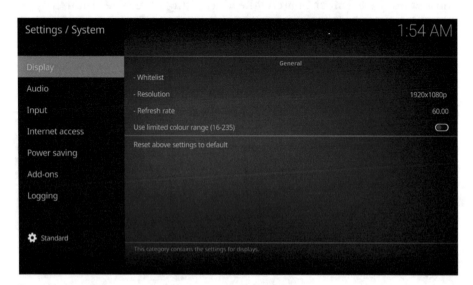

Figure 8-10. *The video resolution settings*

Under Audio you can change the audio output device, with choices for HDMI, 3.5mm jack, and Bluetooth Audio, as shown in Figure 8-11. You can also change volume settings and GUI sound effects.

Figure 8-11. *Available audio devices*

The Input tab lets you change peripheral and control settings. Kodi supports the use of mouse and keyboard, gaming remotes, and traditional remote controls. Basically, if it can connect successfully, then you can use it. If you want to use a keyboard but not a mouse, you can use the arrow keys along with the Enter, backspace, and Esc keys to navigate.

Internet access allows you to further configure your connection settings for more advanced users. Power saving has settings for saving energy, such as putting the display to sleep when the device is not in use, Add-ons has options for updating any add-ons you have installed, and Logging has settings for debugging. If you're interested in tracking event logs and other logs, you'll want to take a closer look at these settings. These logs can be especially helpful if you're planning to contribute to LibreELEC.

LibreELEC Settings

The LibreELEC icon in the bottom-right corner holds a lot of the main system settings. Under System, you can set up backups for Kodi and configure system updates. Network has more advanced Network settings beyond those available under System. Connections shows all the Internet connections available to the Tinker Board, as well as their IP addresses, states and connection types.

The LibreELEC Services are very important. Here you can configure settings for Samba, SSH, Avahi and Bluetooth, as shown in Figure 8-12.

Figure 8-12. *The LibreELEC Services menu*

You'll want to enable Samba, since we'll be using it for sharing files over the network. You'll want to make note of the minimum and maximum supported protocols. By default, the minimum is SMB2 and the maximum is SMB3. Depending on the system you're trying to connect to, you may need to change the minimum support protocol to SMB1.

SSH, of course, allows us to access a terminal to communicate directly with LibreELEC. Be sure to enable this if you need to do that. You would follow the same instructions that we went over when accessing Lakka via SSH. And finally, if you have any Bluetooth devices that you want to use, you'll need to enable Bluetooth at the very bottom of this menu. Otherwise you won't be able to connect. After enabling Bluetooth you'll be able to go to the Bluetooth tab directly underneath Settings to configure any devices, whether they be controllers, speakers, or other items.

Note   To use Bluetooth audio, you'll need to configure it both here and under Audio in the System category that we just went over.

Services

The main feature found in Services that we'll be utilizing is UPnP/ DLNA. Under that section you can enable UPnP (Universal Plug and Play) support and affect settings associated with UPnP. We'll be using UPnP to stream media from a Windows computer later, so if this is of interest to you then you should turn this service on; otherwise it will not work.

The settings for the File Manager, Add-ons, Player, Media, PVR & Live TV, Interface, and Profiles are all meant to customize Kodi to your preferences and needs. As a result, we won't go in-depth for these menus. It's recommended to reference documentation from Kodi to go fully in-depth on everything that is available.

Note   You've probably noticed that a lot of these category and settings names are a bit repetitive, which can be confusing. Once you get more familiar with Kodi, the navigation for settings will become more intuitive.

Loading Media

Now that we've finished going over the settings and getting familiar with the GUI, we can begin loading media into Kodi for playback. There are a few ways to access media with Kodi, with the main differences being that the media will be available either locally to the Tinker Board or remotely over a network connection.

USB Storage

Utilizing a USB drive, whether a flash drive or an external hard drive, is probably the easiest method for accessing media with Kodi. First, you'll need to prepare your files. It's recommended to label all of your media files in a cohesive way and organize them by folder where applicable; especially when separating video files from audio files. Once that's all set, load your files onto your USB device and plug it into one of the Tinker Board's USB ports.

After you connect the drive, a pop-up window will open, asking whether you want to browse videos, music, pictures, or files. You can access your files directly like this or navigate to one of the menu items, such as Movies, and navigate to the drive from there. The menu item categories will show the USB drive with its name next to a small USB port icon, as shown in Figure 8-13. Clicking on it will allow you to go through the file directory of the drive. As long as your USB device remains connected to the Tinker Board, your media will remain accessible in Kodi.

Figure 8-13. *USB storage device connected to the Tinker Board and available as a media source*

Loading Media to Local Storage over the Network

In the previous chapter, we loaded ROMs over the network from a computer to Lakka's file directory. LibreELEC has that same ability using the same steps. First, find your Tinker Board's IP address by navigating to Settings ➤ LibreELEC ➤ Connections or Settings ➤ System Info ➤ Summary. Then, if you haven't already, make sure that Samba is enabled by checking Settings ➤ LibreELEC ➤ Services.

After everything is all set on the Tinker Board side, navigate to your computer's file directory and connect to the Tinker Board using the IP address that we just looked up. After connecting you should see Kodi's file directory, as shown in Figure 8-14.

Figure 8-14. *Kodi's file directory accessed via Samba*

Now you can drag and drop media files to be played locally in Kodi. If you have a USB device connected to the Tinker Board, that device will also show up in the file directory and will have read/write abilities so that you won't have to worry about filling up your SD card or eMMC.

Network Streaming

Network media streaming is more complicated than our previous two methods. Successfully streaming media over the network depends on a variety of factors, including the platform you're streaming from, whether it be Windows, macOS, Linux, or a third-party NAS box. However, network streaming is a big reason to use software like Kodi, especially running on the Tinker Board. When it's running properly, you can have access to your entire media library from a device that fits in the palm of your hand.

There are a few available protocols to create a network connection within Kodi. You can use NFS, SMB, UPnP, or a dedicated server protocol such as FTP or a web server. Here we're going to discuss NFS, SMB, and UPnP.

NFS

NFS stands for Network File System and is available natively in macOS and Linux operating systems. It's also common among NAS setups as well. It is not available on non-server versions of Windows without third-party software. There is a third-party tool called haneWin that Kodi suggests in their documentation if you really want to use NFS on Windows.

macOS NFS Configuration

Both macOS and Linux have similar setup processes for configuring NFS shares. For macOS, open a terminal and enter `sudo nfsd enable` to create an NFS that will reconnect at startup. Next, we need to edit the `/etc/exports` file, which contains the information for which folder is being shared and who the folder is being shared with. Enter `cat /etc/exports` into the terminal and the text file should open. Edit the file using the following syntax:

```
/parentFolder/subFolder -ro -mapall=nobody -alldirs 111.111.1.1
```

Here you're selecting the file path for the folder you want to share and then listing the permissions. For this example, we're using `-ro`, which is read only, `-mapall=nobody`, which allows all users to have the same clearance, and then `-alldirs 111.111.1.1`, which gives access to all the file directories within the specified path if you're accessing it from that IP address; it should be the IP of the Tinker Board.

After you've finished editing `/etc/exports`, save and close the file. Return to the terminal and enter `sudo nfsd restart` to restart the NFS shared folder. Any time you edit `/etc/exports`, you'll need to reboot the server so that the new settings go into effect.

Note   There is also a third-party application available for macOS called NFS Manager that allows you to configure NFS shares through a GUI interface rather than using the terminal.

Linux NFS Configuration

The steps for Linux NFS configuration are very similar to macOS. First open a terminal and install the NFS dependencies by entering sudo apt-get install nfs-kernel-server. There is a chance that this is already installed on your system, but it's better to double-check. Next, edit the /etc/exports file by entering sudo nano /etc/exports. This opens the text file for editing. Specify your configuration using this syntax:

/parentFolder/subFolder 111.111.1.1(rw,all_squash,insecure)

Here, much as in macOS, you're listing the file path for the folder you want to share, followed by the Tinker Board's IP address, and then in parentheses the parameters for the file share. We're using some default options suggested by Kodi in their wiki for NFS that allow for read/write and all UIDs. The insecure parameter allows Kodi to access the folder without root privileges. Notice that there are no spaces between the parentheses or commas.

Save and exit the file by typing control+X, agreeing to save by entering Y. This will bring you back to the terminal. Next, reboot the server to have the changes go into effect by entering sudo service nfs-kernel-server restart. Now we can head back to the Tinker Board to connect to an NFS file share.

Note   If you have a dedicated branded NAS box, NFS should be a viable option for you as well. Check the manufacturer's site for instructions on proper setup. For more common brands, you can also check the Kodi wiki.[5]

---

[5]https://kodi.wiki/view/NFS

Connecting Kodi to an NFS Share

On the main Kodi landing page, select the media type associated with your setup's NFS file share, whether it be movies, music, or whatever. Once in that folder, go down to the bottom of the page and select +Add [videos/music/etc]. This will open a window to add a source, as shown in Figure 8-15. Select the Browse button. This opens a list of available file share types to create a new share. Select Network File System (NFS).

Figure 8-15. *The Add a source window*

After a few seconds, if everything is configured properly, a new window should open, listing the IP address for the device on which you just set up an NFS share. Select that IP address and then click OK. This will bring you back to the original Add source window, this time with your NFS share selected, as shown in Figure 8-16.

Figure 8-16. *The selected NFS share*

The syntax should show nfs://111.111.1.1/. If everything matches, enter a name for the NFS share and click OK at the bottom of the window. You should then see your newly named NFS file share listed as a file source, as shown in Figure 8-17.

Figure 8-17. *NFS file share available as a media source*

Note   The NFS setting examples that were used for both macOS and Linux are not secure. For experimental use they are fine, but for long-term use you'll want to research security settings that are right for your setup.

SMB

We've used Samba both for Lakka and Kodi successfully by easily accessing the file directories for each system from our computers on various operating systems. However, to reverse that process and access a computer from one of these operating systems by setting up a dedicated SMB share to stream media has gotten increasingly difficult in recent years, ever since security vulnerabilities were discovered and operating systems have put in varied security patches.

Additionally, with recent Windows 10 updates discontinuing the use and availability of HomeGroups, beginning with build 1803, it just isn't a recommended option with Kodi. SMB is also slower than other solutions, such as NFS. So it's recommended if you're on macOS or Linux to run an NFS share for network streaming to Kodi. Of course, you can also use the third-party software, haneWin on Windows for NFS access as well. But what if you want to use a dedicated built-in Windows option?

UPnP

UPnP stands for Universal Plug and Play. It's a protocol that's been around for a long time and has its own security concerns, most notably when utilized on routers for port forwarding. The instance of UPnP used by Kodi, though, is a mix of UPnP A/V and DLNA, which is more secure and different from the notorious version seen in many security problems on routers. The solution is not ideal, but on Windows it does work without a lot of effort to set up. If you want to run this long-term, you'll need to take security precautions for your network and check logs often for any abnormalities.

UPnP for Kodi basically prompts you to set up a media streaming server directly on your Windows PC by allowing media streaming services through your network connection. Once it's set up, it's basically the Windows Media Player broadcasting to your Tinker Board. It will automatically grab all your media files from your various folders, and your preexisting folder hierarchies will transfer over to Kodi via your network.

Windows Setup

On your Windows 10 computer, navigate to the Network and Sharing Center in the Control Panel. Select "Change advanced sharing settings," which will bring you to the Advanced Settings page. Here you'll want to turn on the first two options available: Network Discovery and File and Printer Sharing. After enabling both of those options, scroll down to the section that says All Networks. Expand that section and under Media Streaming click "Choose media streaming options," as shown in Figure 8-18.

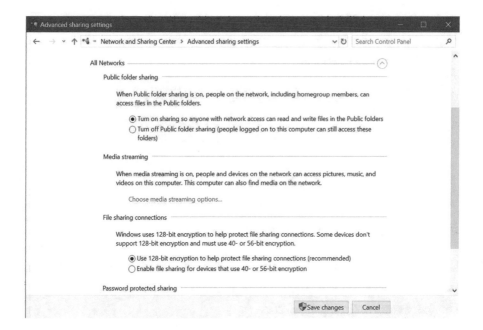

Figure 8-18.   *The All Networks settings area*

A new window will open with a dialog box about media streaming. Click the "Turn on media streaming" button as shown in Figure 8-19. This will open a new window that shows a newly created media library server. You can rename the server to anything you want here. You'll also be able to see other network-connected media devices. If your Tinker Board is on and running Kodi, you will also see a Kodi LibreELEC device. Click OK to save your changes, which will bring you back to the Network Settings page. Double-check that both Network Discovery and File and Printer Sharing are turned on and then click Save Changes to exit the window.

Choose media streaming options for computers and devices

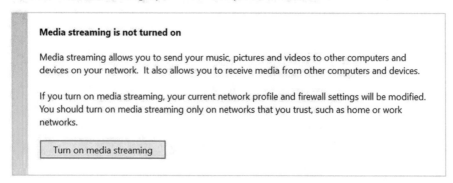

Media streaming is not turned on

Media streaming allows you to send your music, pictures and videos to other computers and devices on your network. It also allows you to receive media from other computers and devices.

If you turn on media streaming, your current network profile and firewall settings will be modified. You should turn on media streaming only on networks that you trust, such as home or work networks.

Turn on media streaming

Figure 8-19. Turning on media streaming

Now navigate to the File Explorer. Click the Network option on the side panel and you should see your newly created media library as a Media Device, as shown in Figure 8-20.

Media Devices (2)

WINDOWSPC: MediaLib:

Figure 8-20. The Media Library listed under Network devices

Connecting UPnP Media Server in Kodi

Before connecting to the shared library, make sure you've enabled UPnP on Kodi by going to Settings ➤ Services ➤ UPnP/DLNA. Then, just as you did setting up NFS in Kodi, navigate to Add a Media Source and click Browse. In the list of new share options, scroll down to the UPnP devices. You should see your Media Library appear in the next window as an option to connect to, as shown in Figure 8-21.

Figure 8-21. *The UPnP devices option under share options*

Once you select the Media Library, you'll be able to target specific folders. It's recommended to map the Music folder to the Music category in Kodi and the Videos folder to the Movies or TV Shows category in Kodi. You can also target specific subfolders as well.

After you select your folder, you'll be brought to the main Add Source window with a upnp:// address specific to your Media Library, as shown in Figure 8-22. Give your source a name and then click OK to connect to the Media Library. After that you'll see it as an option in your media list.

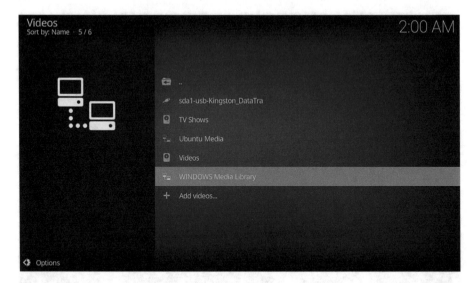

Figure 8-22. *The Media Library configured and ready to be added as a UPnP device in Kodi*

Note   If you don't see your media library under UPnP devices in Kodi, ensure that your computer with the shared Media Library is turned on and connected to the network. Then ensure that the Tinker Board is connected to the network. If neither of those things are an issue, try rebooting the Tinker Board. If the Media Library doesn't show up after that, navigate to Settings ➤ Services ➤ UPnP and toggle it off and then on. You should be able to select the Media Library now.

Conclusion

We've gone over a lot in this chapter, from cross-compiling to build an ISO, to taking a tour of Kodi and setting up multiple types of network shares on different operating systems. There is still a lot more that we could go over with Kodi, but this chapter should get you well on your way to building a dedicated media center with the Tinker Board. The Tinker Board's hardware and specs make it a great choice for a dedicated media center, especially one with network capabilities. The added 4K capabilities will certainly be a great bonus for video enthusiasts.

We shouldn't forget about the audiophiles among us either, though; and while Kodi certainly has great options for music, there is a dedicated audio playback Linux distro that we can integrate with high quality DACs that fit directly onto the GPIO pins. Let's continue our specialized Linux distro tour with Volumio!

CHAPTER 9

Project 3: Stream Music to the Tinker Board with Volumio

Our third project will be the final one that focuses on media consumption and a specialized operating system. We'll be using Volumio to set up the Tinker Board as an audio streaming device.

But what is Volumio? Volumio is a specialized Linux distribution built on Debian for audio playback for a variety of file formats. It can play files that are stored locally or on a network drive, and even stream them from another device. It's meant to be used as a *headless* device, meaning that it shouldn't have a display or keyboard attached. Instead, Volumio is controlled remotely through a browser interface. It can also be accessed via SSH, which we explored in both the Lakka and Kodi projects.

With Volumio, you can use a variety of different outputs on the Tinker Board for playback. You can use the native outputs of either the headphone jack or HDMI, of course, but you can also use a USB-powered DAC or an I2S-based audio HAT ("Hardware attached on top") that sits on the GPIO pins. The ability to use I2S is a big reason to use Volumio for your audio. I2S (inter-IC sound) is a serial bus interface that enables PCM audio data to be communicated between integrated circuits. Because of how the sound data is transmitted with separate clock and data feeds, I2S results in high-quality audio.

© Liz Clark 2019
L. Clark, *Practical Tinker Board*, https://doi.org/10.1007/978-1-4842-3826-4_9

Support for the Tinker Board

Unlike the last two operating systems that we looked at, Volumio has an official release for the Tinker Board that is fully supported. As a result, we can easily download the ISO for it from Volumio's web site. We can also check for any updates and peruse the forums for any issues people are having. Additionally, there are supported I2S audio DAC HATs that can be used with the Tinker Board, specifically the HiFiBerry series of I2S DACs and the IQaudIO DAC Plus, which also utilizes I2S.

We'll be looking at the HiFiBerry+ DAC and the IQaudIO DAC Plus for use with Volumio on the Tinker Board. The HiFiBerry+ has only RCA connectors for audio output, as shown in Figure 9-1.

Figure 9-1. *The HiFiBerry+ RCA DAC HAT*

Even though it has a spot for a 3.5mm headphone jack to be added to the board, further modification is needed to support the circuit fully.[1] The IQaudIO DAC Plus has both RCA and a headphone jack for outputs, which you can see in Figure 9-2.

Figure 9-2. *The IQaudIO DAC Plus HAT. Notice that it has both RCA and headphone outputs.*

Both HATs have headers that just clear the stock Tinker Board heatsink, so both can be used without modification or stacking headers. Which one you choose will depend on your audio needs and personal preference. You can see a side-by-side comparison of both HATs in Figure 9-3.

---

[1]Some basic documentation on adding a headphone jack option to the RCA version of the HiFiBerry+ DAC from the HiFiBerry forum: https://support.hifiberry.com/hc/en-us/community/posts/115002245989-DAC-HW-2-3-cannot-use-phone-jack

Figure 9-3. *The HiFiBerry+ RCA DAC HAT and the IQaudIO DAC Plus HAT. The main differences between the two are in the audio output options.*

Installing the Volumio Disk Image

As previously stated, there is an official Volumio release for the Tinker Board, which means that we can go directly to the Volumio web site and download the disk image. Navigate to www.volumio.org and click the Download tab at the top of the page. This will bring you to the disk image downloads page, where disk images are available for multiple platforms. Select ASUS Tinker Board from the list and then click the Download icon as shown in Figure 9-4.

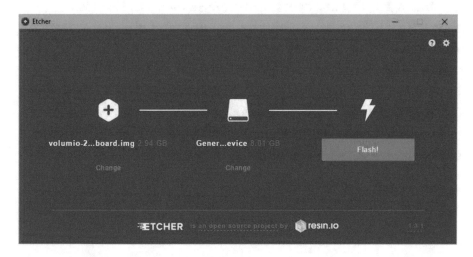

DOWNLOAD VOLUMIO FOR YOUR PLATFORM

RASPBERRY PI

PC (X86/X64)

ODROID C1

ODROID C2

SPARKY

ASUS TINKERBOARD

Volumio Audiophile Music Player for ASUS Tinkerboard

VERSION: 2.411

RELEASE DATE: 15-06-2018

TOTAL DOWNLOADS: 49548

IMAGE MD5: 2cfa4129d1b156dd297fdfbfac7f6131

CHANGELOG LINK

DOWNLOAD

Figure 9-4.   *The Volumio disk image that is available for download for the Tinker Board*

After downloading the ISO file, prepare your storage as outlined previously in Chapter 3 and open Etcher to burn the Volumio ISO to your chosen storage device, either an SD card or the eMMC on the Tinker Board S, as shown in Figure 9-5.

Figure 9-5.   *The Volumio ISO being burned to a storage device with Etcher*

First Boot

Before you power up your Tinker Board with Volumio for the first time, it's incredibly important to first attach all the necessary peripherals. You'll of course need your power supply, but you will also need to attach your chosen audio playback method and a wired Ethernet connection for Internet connectivity.

During the first boot, the file system for Volumio is resized, and it looks for connected peripherals to the Tinker Board to configure settings. For example, if you attach an HDMI cable during the first boot, but not your audio HAT, Volumio will think that you want to utilize the HDMI output for audio and it will also disable the on-board headphone jack, which will make changing settings using the browser controller a bit difficult.

The wired Internet connection is needed because all control for Volumio takes place via a browser GUI interface. Here you can set up a wireless connection, which we'll go over shortly, but that wired connection is needed to start. Once all these connections are ready, you can power-on the Tinker Board to begin using Volumio.

Once again, that first boot will take longer than usual to finish because of the file system resizing process that takes place; an event that we've experienced with other operating systems as well. Once it finishes booting, you can navigate to volumio.local in a browser on a device that is connected to the same network as the Tinker Board. You should see a GUI control interface for Volumio, as shown in Figure 9-6. If you don't see it, then either it hasn't finished booting yet or there's a problem, such as a disconnected network connection or, more rarely, a corrupt install of Volumio.

Figure 9-6. *The landing page for the Volumio browser GUI*

Configure Playback and Wi-Fi

From volumio.local, we're going to finish the setup for Volumio, specifically connecting to Wi-Fi and configuring our playback device. Then we'll reboot the system before beginning general use. Both the network and playback options are located under Settings, which can be accessed via the cog icon in the top-right corner. After you click it, a dropdown menu as shown in Figure 9-7 will appear with all the various settings available.

MY MUSIC   ✕

PLAYBACK OPTIONS

APPEARANCE

NETWORK

SYSTEM

PLUGINS

ALARM

SLEEP

SHUTDOWN

VOLUMIO SHOP

Figure 9-7. *The Settings menu. Most options can be accessed through this menu.*

For Wi-Fi setup, select Network from the Settings dropdown. This will bring you to all the available Network settings. If you scroll to the middle of the page you'll see a list of available wireless networks, as shown in Figure 9-8. Select your network and then click Connect. You'll then be prompted for your password and be able to click Connect again. After this, you should be connected to your Wi-Fi network.

Figure 9-8. *The available wireless networks under Network settings*

Volumio functions well with Wi-Fi, since streaming music does not require as much bandwidth as video streaming. However, if your goal with Volumio is to stream music with a high bit rate and depth, then you may want to consider continuing a wired connection. This will also help to prevent any connectivity issues that can happen with Wi-Fi streaming.

Next, we need to set up our audio output. In the Settings menu, select Playback Options. At the very top of that page you'll see the Audio Output options. From the first dropdown menu, select the type of device you're using.

If you are using I2S, you'll also need to toggle the I2S DAC option to On and then select your DAC HAT from the second dropdown menu, as shown in Figure 9-9.

Figure 9-9. *The I2S DAC options under playback*

After selecting your options, reboot the Tinker Board via `volumio.local` by going back to Settings and selecting Shutdown toward the bottom of the list. This will open a pop-up style window with options for Power Off and Restart, as well as an option to Cancel, as shown in Figure 9-10. Select Restart and after about a minute you'll be able to log in to Volumio via `volumio.local` again.

Figure 9-10. *The power options that are available after selecting Shutdown*

Once the reboot has been completed successfully, navigate back to Playback Options to confirm that your audio output settings are correct. After reboot, if you're using an I2S DAC, your I2S DAC model will appear as the option in the first dropdown, as shown in Figure 9-11.

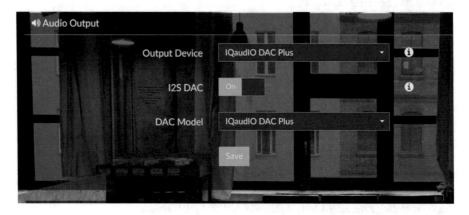

Figure 9-11. *The I2S DAC audio output fully configured after reboot*

Navigating the Browser GUI

Now that your basic setup is taken care of, we can take a quick tour of volumio.local to get a feel for the controls and options that Volumio offers. The browser interface is where you'll be able to control all the basic options for Volumio, including playback and file access options.

The default page for `volumio.local` is the Playback page, which will show you what audio is currently playing, or after a reboot/shutdown what the last audio played was. You'll also have options for volume and normal media controls for play, pause, stop, and so on. At the bottom of the page are three tabs: Browse, Playback, and Queue. Playback will bring you back to the main page, and Queue allows you to queue up audio playlists for playback. The Browse tab is where you can access your available audio files, whether they are locally stored, streamed, or even Internet radio, as shown in Figure 9-12.

Figure 9-12. *The file options available in the Browse tab*

Local and network drive files can be sorted by the entire music library, artists, albums or genres. You can also favorite tracks to create a compilation of tracks that are sorted in Volumio. For local storage, you'll simply attach a drive via USB, as we did with Kodi and Lakka. For accessing a network drive, though, there's a little bit more setup involved.

To configure a network drive or Network Attached Storage (NAS), you'll need to go to Settings and then My Music. As shown in Figure 9-13, this will bring you to a page where you can name your NAS, enter its IP address, and then configure the file path to allow Volumio access to where your audio files are stored. Their files will now show-up under the Browse tab along with the locally stored files.

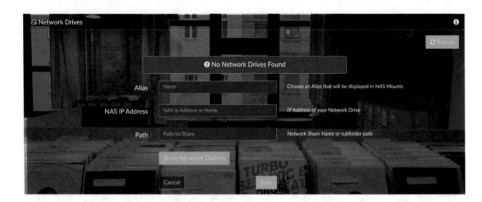

Figure 9-13. *The NAS configuration setup*

UPnP and Internet Radio

There are a few more options for playing back audio as well. We discussed a couple of network streaming options in the previous chapter; and much like Kodi, Volumio supports UPnP media server streaming. You can reference the setup steps for Kodi in Chapter 8 to use them with Volumio. Better yet, if you still have your UPnP server set up from the Kodi chapter, it should appear as a Media Server option, as shown in Figure 9-14.

Figure 9-14. *A UPnP Media Server available in Volumio. This particular server was set up for Kodi in Chapter 8.*

Volumio also has built-in access to Internet Radio stations of multiple genres, as shown in Figure 9-15.

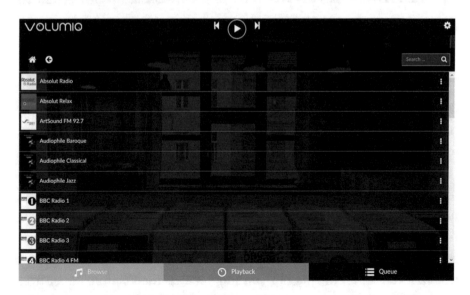

Figure 9-15. *Some of the Internet Radio stations available with Volumio*

These are accessed through the Web Radio option under Volumio Selection. You simply click on a station to begin streaming. A BBC station can be seen streaming in Figure 9-16.

Figure 9-16. An Internet Radio station streaming with Volumio

Streaming via Airplay

One of the biggest features of Volumio is its ability to receive audio via AirPlay. This means that you can stream audio from your phone, laptop, tablet, or other device to Volumio.

But first, what is AirPlay? It is a proprietary protocol from Apple that allows you to stream between devices. Currently, AirPlay allows more than just audio streaming, but for our purposes we'll concentrate on audio. AirPlay is a built-in feature on all Apple devices, but it is also available via secondary software for Windows PCs and Android devices. When you send a stream via AirPlay to Volumio, you simply select the Volumio device from the AirPlay menu, as shown in Figure 9-17, and it will begin streaming to the Tinker Board.

Figure 9-17. *An example of Volumio being available as an AirPlay device*

Issues with AirPlay

One problem that can occur with AirPlay is that sometimes there can be delays or random pauses and glitches with the audio playback. This can be caused by a variety of factors, including Internet bandwidth, device speeds, the size of the file being streamed, and software settings.

Particularly in Volumio, one setting you can adjust is the audio buffer size. A larger buffer will mean that a larger portion of the audio file will be buffered, or loaded, and ready to play, decreasing the chance of an audio file constantly starting and stopping. It does cause a delay in a file beginning to play, but it at least increases the likelihood of a successful overall listening experience.

If, however, after checking all the variables you're still experiencing issues, we can edit the ALSA audio settings within Volumio to fix the issues once and for all. This also gives us the opportunity to try SSH with Volumio and experience the back-end of the distro.

Connecting to Volumio with SSH

To be able to connect via SSH, we need to first enable SSH. This is done through a secondary browser interface for Volumio, which can be accessed in a browser with `volumio.local/dev`. This will bring you to a simplified GUI that has a lot of debugging information, as well as an option to enable SSH, as shown in Figure 9-18.

Figure 9-18. *The volumio.local/dev browser page. Notice the toggle for SSH.*

After enabling SSH, we're going to use either PuTTY on Windows or the terminal on macOS and Linux to access Volumio, the same way we accessed Lakka with SSH in Chapter 7. To connect, we'll need the Tinker Board's IP address, which can be located with `volumio.local` under Network Settings.

Once you connect with SSH, you'll be prompted for a login. The default username for Volumio is volumio and the default password is also volumio, as shown in Figure 9-19.

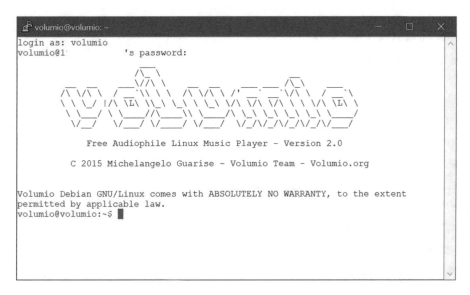

Figure 9-19. *The default login via SSH for Volumio*

You'll want to change these if you plan to leave SSH enabled or be sure to disable SSH after you're finished, for security reasons. We're going to be editing an AirPlay configuration file[2] with the nano text editor to fine-tune the ALSA audio settings to limit the latency that's causing the AirPlay audio glitches. To do this, while connected via SSH, enter

```
nano /volumio/app/plugins/music_service/airplay_emulation/
shairport-sync.conf.tmpl
```

---

[2]This fix was found on a webpage that was linked in the Volumio forum as a solution for AirPlay issues: http://nw-electric.way-nifty.com/blog/2017/03/shairport-sync-.html

Inside the text file, edit the following lines to read as shown:

```
general =
{
name = "${name}";
interpolation = "soxr";
log_verbosity = 0;
};
alsa =
{
output_device = "hw:1,0";
mixer_device = "hw:1";
mixer_control_name = "Digital";
output_format = "S32";
output_rate=44100;
period_size=4410;
buffer_size=22050;
};
sessioncontrol =
{
run_this_before_play_begins = "/usr/bin/mpc stop";
allow_session_interruption = "yes";
};
```

After your edits are complete, save the file and then reboot from SSH using reboot to apply the changes. To test, try streaming via AirPlay to Volumio. If the fix was successful, you should notice that any playback glitches have been eliminated.

Finishing Touches

Once you've gotten Volumio all set up and have tested out your preferred options for audio playback, you may want to consider a case for your Tinker Board if it will be acting as a dedicated Volumio player. If you're utilizing a DAC HAT, there are specialized cases available for use with most HATs on the market. If you can't find one for your DAC HAT, you can also utilize a case that is designed for use with HATs in general, as long as it has access to the top to allow for the audio output connectors.

With a Wi-Fi connection, you'll only need to connect power to the Tinker Board, meaning that it can operate without any other peripherals attached. As mentioned at the beginning of this chapter, a computer used this way is referred to as headless. Our next two projects will also have the Tinker Board operate as headless. Being able to use the Tinker Board this way makes it very convenient for standalone applications and adds to its versatility for projects. An additional benefit to being headless is that it can be kept discretely near your speakers or inside your media center.

Conclusion

We've now gone over three media projects, a genre that the Tinker Board really excels at thanks to its hardware specs, community support and software development. For our final two projects, we're going to move on and branch out to different types of projects that will bring us back to TinkerOS and integrate some Python programming.

CHAPTER 10

Project 4: Using an e-Paper Display for Weather Data

After going over some specialized distributions of Linux for the Tinker Board, it's time to return to where this book began: TinkerOS. This time around, we're going to be applying the Linux, GPIO, and programming skills that we gained in the first part of the book. The first project that we'll tackle is an Internet-connected display with an e-Paper module that will show the current date, time, and weather.

What Is e-Paper?

Often referred to as e-Ink or EPD, e-Paper (electronic paper) is a digital display that mimics the look of ink on paper. It's the same type of display found in e-readers and other similar devices. It has a slow refresh rate, so it's best for static displays, such as images or slowly changing text. Because of this, it has incredibly low power consumption. e-Paper is also known for being easily visible in all lighting conditions, including direct sunlight, and it's easier on your eyes because it doesn't emit the blue light found in LCD displays.

© Liz Clark 2019
L. Clark, *Practical Tinker Board*, https://doi.org/10.1007/978-1-4842-3826-4_10

e-Paper comes in a variety of shapes and sizes. Traditionally, the displays are dual-color; usually black and white, but newer versions can showcase other colors, and tricolor displays are also beginning to come to market. They're becoming increasingly popular for DIY applications, since they're available for multiple platforms. Many displays can be coded in multiple coding languages with manufacturer-provided libraries that you can install, along with example code to test included. They usually connect through individual broken-out pins to attach to GPIO pins on different boards, but there are also specialized add-on boards that fit directly onto certain boards' GPIO layouts, including the Tinker Board.

The display that we're going to use for this project is from Waveshare, a manufacturer of DIY electronics accessories. They have quite a few varieties of e-Paper displays available, and the one we'll be looking at is the 2.13-inch HAT variety. It was originally designed to work with Raspberry Pi, but ASUS has ported the Python libraries to work with the Tinker Board so that no code adjustment is needed. We'll examine what they did, though, so that you can try porting hardware libraries for future projects.

SPI

You may be wondering how the e-Paper displays work. Some, including the one we'll be using, use Serial Peripheral Interface (SPI) communication. SPI is a bus protocol used to communicate between devices. It has a built-in clock signal that is sent in conjunction with any data for highly accurate and timely communication. SPI is integrated into Python using the `spidev` library, which we'll discuss shortly as we prepare for the Waveshare library installation.

Early Issues with SPI on the Tinker Board

Previously, there were some issues with SPI on the Tinker Board. Although both the original Tinker Board and Tinker Board S have two SPI controllers, SPI0 and SPI2, available via the GPIO, only SPI2 was enabled at the kernel level. Beginning with TinkerOS 2.0.7, this issue has been resolved and now both SPI0 and SPI2 can be utilized. This increases compatibility with a lot of hardware.

To ensure that your chosen SPI controller is enabled, navigate to a terminal in TinkerOS and enter sudo nano /boot/hw_intf.conf to edit the text file for I2C and SPI communication settings. Once in the nano file, simply change the setting next to the different functions from Off to On by typing, as shown in Figure 10-1, and then save the file. You'll need to reboot to finish enabling SPI or other protocols. It's important to note that some GPIO pins control multiple functions; and by enabling functions that share pins, you may run into some issues. To play it safe, only enable the ones that you need at the time and always refer to the pinout to double-check.

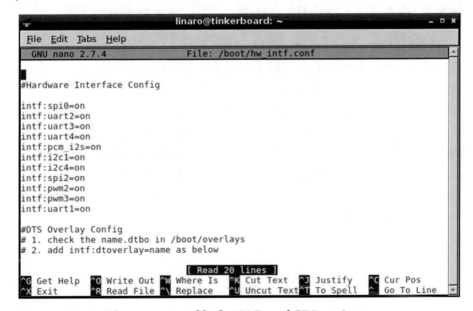

Figure 10-1. *The nano text file for I2C and SPI settings*

The e-Paper Display's Hardware

The e-Paper display that we will use has two major parts: the actual display and the PCB HAT. The display has a short ribbon cable that plugs into the side of the HAT, as shown in Figure 10-2. The HAT then breaks out the signals from the ribbon cable to the components on the board and eventually the GPIO pins.

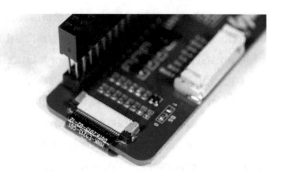

Figure 10-2. *The EPD's ribbon cable that connects to the HAT*

This HAT also has a separate breakout connector to connect the individual signals in lieu of using the 40-pin GPIO header that you can also observe in Figure 10-2. You'd use this with other types of development boards or if you didn't want the display to sit directly on top of the Tinker Board, depending on your project's housing. Coincidentally, the 40-pin header is a bit short for this display and can't clear the stock heat sink for the Tinker Board. You can use a 40-pin header to act as a riser so that the HAT can comfortably fit on the Tinker Board with the heat sink as shown in Figure 10-3.

Figure 10-3. *The 40-pin header being used as a riser for the 2.13-inch EPD HAT*

Setting Up the EPD's Software

As mentioned previously, we're going to use the EPD with TinkerOS. Boot into TinkerOS and then navigate to the terminal so that we can begin installing the Python dependencies.

First, make sure you're in the Home directory by changing directories with `cd ~`, and then run `sudo apt-get update` followed by

```
sudo apt-get install python-dev python-setuptools python-pip
python-wheel python-pil
```

`pip` is a package management system that allows you to install Python dependencies, tools and libraries for Python, similar to using `apt-get install` or `git` for other programs and downloads in Linux. However, best results for installation occur when you're targeting the Home directory. Using `pip,` we're going to install the SPI library by entering `pip install spidev` into the terminal. After that, run `sudo apt-get upgrade` and `sudo reboot`.

Note   Some dependencies, like `python-dev`, were installed during other chapters. They're repeated here in case you didn't follow directly along with those chapters. Trying to install them again won't damage your build of TinkerOS; they'll just be ignored.

Next, we'll install the libraries for this display. As discussed, Waveshare has many different e-Paper displays, and they all have different libraries, meaning that one display's library will not work with another. Specifically, for our display, you'll remember that there is a ported version of the library so that it will work with the Tinker Board, which was developed by a member of the ASUS team. This ported version is currently hosted on the Tinker Board's wiki site in a 7zip folder,[1] as shown in Figure 10-4.

Attachment

Media:TB sample code.7z

Figure 10-4. *The 7zip file hosted on the Tinker Board wiki site for Waveshare add-ons. It's located at the very bottom of the web page, which is linked in Footnote 1.*

You can download and unzip the folder either on your main computer or on the Tinker Board. If you access it with the Tinker Board, best results for unzipping were experienced using the GUI tools rather than the terminal since it's a 7zip folder rather than a zip folder. Once you open the folder, you'll see files labeled epd2in13.py, epdif.py, main.py, and monocolor.bmp. The epd2in13.py and epdif.py files are the library files. You'll need to have these files in the same folder as your Python program for the display so that it runs properly. The main.py file is a demo program

---

[1]https://tinkerboarding.co.uk/wiki/index.php/Waveshare-Expansions Scroll down to the bottom of the page to locate the folder, as shown in Figure 10-4.

for the display, and `monocolor.bmp` is a bitmap picture formatted to appear properly on the display. The `main.py` program has some lines of code that call for this bitmap to be displayed.

Ported Libraries

Before we see the final result of these ported libraries, let's see what makes them tick. Studying these will also help in understanding how to get started with porting code and libraries to the Tinker Board later.

First, let's look at `epdif.py`. We'll do that by first changing directories to the newly unzipped folder and then entering `idle epdif.py` into the terminal. This opens any file with IDLE. Looking at the beginning of the file, as shown in Figure 10-5, we see some libraries being imported; the most notable is `import ASUS.GPIO as GPIO`. Previously this would have been calling for the import of the Raspberry Pi GPIO library. When adjusting code or libraries for the Tinker Board, this will be one of the easiest and most important changes to make.

```
epdif.py - /home/linaro/gpio_lib_python/networkStart/epdif.py (2.7.13)      - □ ×

File  Edit  Format  Run  Options  Window  Help

#   @author        :    Yehui from Waveshare
#
#   Copyright (C) Waveshare      July 10 2017
#
# Permission is hereby granted, free of charge, to any person obtaining a copy
# of this software and associated documnetation files (the "Software"), to deal
# in the Software without restriction, including without limitation the rights
# to use, copy, modify, merge, publish, distribute, sublicense, and/or sell
# copies of the Software, and to permit persons to  whom the Software is
# furished to do so, subject to the following conditions:
#
# The above copyright notice and this permission notice shall be included in
# all copies or substantial portions of the Software.
#
# THE SOFTWARE IS PROVIDED "AS IS", WITHOUT WARRANTY OF ANY KIND, EXPRESS OR
# IMPLIED, INCLUDING BUT NOT LIMITED TO THE WARRANTIES OF MERCHANTABILITY,
# FITNESS OR A PARTICULAR PURPOSE AND NONINFRINGEMENT. IN NO EVENT SHALL THE
# AUTHORS OR COPYRIGHT HOLDERS BE LIABLE FOR ANY CLAIM, DAMAGES OR OTHER
# LIABILITY WHETHER IN AN ACTION OF CONTRACT, TORT OR OTHERWISE, ARISING FROM,
# OUT OF OR IN CONNECTION WITH THE SOFTWARE OR THE USE OR OTHER DEALINGS IN
# THE SOFTWARE.
#

import spidev
import ASUS.GPIO as GPIO
import time

# Pin definition
RST_PIN         = 11
DC_PIN          = 22
CS_PIN          = 24
BUSY_PIN        = 18

# SPI device, bus = 0, device = 0
SPI = spidev.SpiDev(2, 0)

def epd_digital_write(pin, value):
    GPIO.output(pin, value)

def epd_digital_read(pin):
    return GPIO.input(BUSY_PIN)

def epd_delay_ms(delaytime):
    time.sleep(delaytime / 1000.0)

def spi_transfer(data):
    SPI.writebytes(data)

def epd_init():
    GPIO.setmode(GPIO.BOARD)
    GPIO.setwarnings(False)
    GPIO.setup(RST_PIN, GPIO.OUT)
    GPIO.setup(DC_PIN, GPIO.OUT)
    GPIO.setup(CS_PIN, GPIO.OUT)
    GPIO.setup(BUSY_PIN, GPIO.IN)
    SPI.max_speed_hz = 2000000
    SPI.mode = 0b00
    return 0;

### END OF FILE ###

                                                              Ln: 1   Col: 0
```

Figure 10-5. *The* epdif.py *file. You can reference this figure for the entire discussion of the* epdif.py *file.*

Looking further, we can also see that the spidev library is being imported here, which implies that SPI settings along with GPIO settings will be taken care of with this file. Sure enough, the next section of code defines the pins needed from the GPIO for SPI. Pins for Reset, DC (Data/Command control), CS (SPI chip select), and Busy (Busy state output) for the e-Paper display are assigned to the proper Tinker Board physical board pins. This is another item you'll want to check, since many Raspberry Pi libraries utilize a different numbering convention.

Next, we see SPI being set up to run with the SPI2 bus by calling spidev.SpiDev(2, 0). If you wanted to change this to run on SPI0, you'd call spidev.SpiDev(0, 0).

Following SPI, we have some digital_write and digital_read functions for the GPIO pins that were previously defined. But the most notable and important function is epd.init(), which will be called for most major commands with the e-Paper display. It basically finishes setting up the GPIO pins and then resets them to their default states. You can see the call for the GPIO.Board numbering convention, followed by code that sets Reset, DC, and CS as outputs and Busy as an input. You can also see that the SPI speed and mode are defined as well. Later, when you see epd.init() called, know that this process is happening along with the other parameter that will be inside the parentheses.

Technically these functions and definitions could be written in your main code, but it would make your code very long, possibly create conflicts, and slow things down. The purpose of libraries and dependency files is to take care of a lot of the back-end prep aspects of code so that it can simply be referenced in the main code file.

The Second Library File

After finishing up with epdif.py, we can look at the second and final library file, ep2in13.py, by entering idle ep2in13.py into the terminal. The name refers to the official name of the EPD and contains a lot of driver communication for the display.

In Figure 10-6, the first lines we see are again importing libraries. We can see import ASUS.GPIO as GPIO, since there are some GPIO commands in this file. It also imports the epdif.py file that we just looked at, so it can utilize the functions and previously defined GPIO parameters. It imports the PIL library as well, which we'll discuss shortly when we look at the demo code.

```
import epdif
from PIL import Image
import ASUS.GPIO as GPIO

# Display resolution
EPD_WIDTH       = 128
EPD_HEIGHT      = 250
```

Figure 10-6. *The top of the ep2in13.py file*

The other major adjustable item is the screen resolution, defined directly under the library imports. The resolution for this display is set to 128 pixels wide and 250 pixels high. This means that the driver and library consider this to be a vertical display. We'll want to change the display to show horizontally for our project, but we'll take care of that in our main code rather than here, since the driver and other library dependencies are written with a vertical orientation in mind.

The rest of the file contains the library commands and functions that make it easier to communicate succinctly with the display, some of which we'll see shortly in the demo code. You can also reference this file to see if there are any additional functions that will be beneficial to your code or to create your own functions. Many of these will be nested in the epd.init() function as well.

Demo Code

To run the demo code, attach the EPD HAT to the Tinker Board's GPIO pins and then navigate to the folder with your Waveshare files. For the purposes of the tutorial, let's assume that they're in a folder called Waveshare in the Home directory. To navigate to the folder, enter cd / home/linaro/Waveshare into the terminal. Now, to run the demo code, enter sudo python main.py into the terminal. Your e-Paper display should blink black and white three times and then begin showing lines and words, followed by the image seen in the bitmap file, as shown in Figure 10-7.

Figure 10-7. *The bitmap file showing on the EPD HAT while the included demo code runs*

Running the demo code should give you an idea of what these displays are capable of. Knowing what's included in the libraries now, let's take a closer look at main.py to understand how the program code is structured and how we'll be able to write our own code for our display project.

Open main.py through the terminal with idle main.py. Once it opens, you'll see that it's structured very similarly to the Python programs that we wrote in the GPIO chapter, as shown in Figure 10-8. First, we have the dependencies, beginning with epd2in13, which we just looked at, followed by the time library and Image, ImageDraw and ImageFont portions of the PIL library.

```
import epd2in13
import time
from PIL import Image
from PIL import ImageDraw
from PIL import ImageFont

def main():
    epd = epd2in13.EPD()
    epd.init(epd.lut_full_update)

    # For simplicity, the arguments are explicit numerical coordinates
    image = Image.new('1', (epd2in13.EPD_WIDTH, epd2in13.EPD_HEIGHT), 255)  # 255: clear the frame
    draw = ImageDraw.Draw(image)
    font = ImageFont.truetype('/usr/share/fonts/truetype/freefont/FreeMonoBold.ttf', 12)
    draw.rectangle((0, 76, 176, 96), fill = 0)
    draw.text((18, 80), 'Hello world!', font = font, fill = 255)
    draw.text((20, 50), 'e-Paper Demo', font = font, fill = 0)
    draw.line((10, 130, 10, 180), fill = 0)
    draw.line((10, 130, 50, 130), fill = 0)
    draw.line((50, 130, 50, 180), fill = 0)
    draw.line((10, 180, 50, 180), fill = 0)
    draw.line((10, 130, 50, 180), fill = 0)
    draw.line((50, 130, 10, 180), fill = 0)
    draw.arc((90, 190, 150, 250), 0, 360, fill = 0)
    draw.chord((90, 120, 150, 180), 0, 360, fill = 0)
    draw.rectangle((10, 200, 50, 250), fill = 0)

    epd.clear_frame_memory(0xFF)
    epd.set_frame_memory(image, 0, 0)
    epd.display_frame()

    epd.delay_ms(2000)

    # for partial update
    epd.init(epd.lut_partial_update)
    image = Image.open('monocolor.bmp')
##
# there are 2 memory areas embedded in the e-paper display
# and once the display is refreshed, the memory area will be auto-toggled,
# i.e. the next action of SetFrameMemory will set the other memory area
# therefore you have to set the frame memory twice.
##
    epd.set_frame_memory(image, 0, 0)
    epd.display_frame()
    epd.set_frame_memory(image, 0, 0)
    epd.display_frame()

    time_image = Image.new('1', (96, 32), 255)  # 255: clear the frame
    draw = ImageDraw.Draw(time_image)
    font = ImageFont.truetype('/usr/share/fonts/truetype/freefont/FreeMonoBold.ttf', 32)
    image_width, image_height = time_image.size
    while (True):
        # draw a rectangle to clear the image
        draw.rectangle((0, 0, image_width, image_height), fill = 255)
        draw.text((0, 0), time.strftime('%M:%S'), font = font, fill = 0)
        epd.display_frame()

if __name__ == '__main__':
    main()
```

Figure 10-8. *The main.py demo code file*

The PIL library was mentioned briefly when we saw it imported in the ep2in13.py file. PIL is the Python Imaging Library. It's an image-processing library that allows you to manipulate images in a variety of ways, including editing pixels with the ImageDraw portion of the library. The current form of PIL is actually a fork of the original library called

Pillow[2] and is widely used in a variety of applications. Beyond the hardware and SPI communication, it's basically the backbone of the EPD since it allows for the hard-coded images and imported image files to be displayed and controlled.

Then we move on to main(), where the bulk of the code lives. First, epd is defined as epd2in13.EPD(), referring to the library file, and then the display is initialized with a full update by calling epd.init(epd.lut_full_update), which results in the screen flashing black and white a few times when starting main.py.

The next part of the code looks very dense, but if we break it apart it will begin to make sense and not seem so intimidating. This section (Figure 10-9) is where all the items that you see on the screen while main.py is running, except for the bitmap file, are programmed. We'll be writing similar code for our project, so seeing and understanding this syntax will definitely make things easier.

```
# For simplicity, the arguments are explicit numerical coordinates
image = Image.new('1', (epd2in13.EPD_WIDTH, epd2in13.EPD_HEIGHT), 255)  # 255: clear the frame
draw = ImageDraw.Draw(image)
font = ImageFont.truetype('/usr/share/fonts/truetype/freefont/FreeMonoBold.ttf', 12)
draw.rectangle((0, 76, 176, 96), fill = 0)
draw.text((18, 80), 'Hello world!', font = font, fill = 255)
draw.text((20, 50), 'e-Paper Demo', font = font, fill = 0)
draw.line((10, 130, 10, 180), fill = 0)
draw.line((10, 130, 50, 130), fill = 0)
draw.line((50, 130, 50, 180), fill = 0)
draw.line((10, 180, 50, 180), fill = 0)
draw.line((10, 130, 50, 180), fill = 0)
draw.line((50, 130, 10, 180), fill = 0)
draw.arc((90, 190, 150, 250), 0, 360, fill = 0)
draw.chord((90, 120, 150, 180), 0, 360, fill = 0)
draw.rectangle((10, 200, 50, 250), fill = 0)
```

Figure 10-9. *The lines of code that create the first image drawn for the demo code*

The first three lines in this block of code define image, draw, and font, which will be called throughout the script. The image parameter is used to refer to everything drawn on the display. For example, if you program

---

[2]For more information on Pillow: https://pillow.readthedocs.io/en/5.2.x/

three circles and a word to appear together, it is defined as an image and is created by calling image.new. The other parameters defined here are the size of the image (usually matching the resolution listed in the library, as we saw in epd2in13.py) and the color, which is expressed as a number. Here it's entered as 255, which is white. For this library, 0 will mean black and 255 will mean white. When setting up an image, always call 255 so that the frame can be cleared as commented in the code.

The draw method is called to "draw" the image. By "drawing," it's sending data to the screen as interpreted from all the parameters that are called later in conjunction with draw.object(). Finally, font is used to pull a font library from a file directory in TinkerOS to be used for drawing strings. For each font that you use you'll need to create a new font object. The font size is also defined after the file directory position, as shown in Figure 10-9.

The remaining lines in the block are the items that appear on the screen, programmed one item at a time using draw.rectangle, draw.text, draw.line, draw.arc, and draw.chord, which is a circle. For the shapes and lines, the four numbers in the parentheses are coordinates for their origin and end points using an (x, y, x, y) format. Since they are being "drawn," you're essentially telling the PIL library to send the pixels with the coordinates acting as a map. The fill parameter is for color, calling for a number between 0 and 255. The chord and arc shapes have an extra parameter for degrees in a range of 0 to 360.

text is set up a bit differently than the shapes. It only has one set of coordinates, which represent the starting point. This is followed by the string that will be written to the screen. Finally, the font is defined along with the fill color.

Note   Keep track of commas and parentheses when creating these items in your code. The syntax is very important and very particular.

The remainder of main() contains the more technical aspects of the code, controlling how the EPD properly shows the data. The first three commands, clear_frame_memory, set_frame_memory and display_ frame() are called immediately after the image is written. The HAT has two memory banks to store the data that it receives from the Tinker Board, and they need to be manually cleared and refreshed. clear_frame_memory completely erases both memory banks and is called only once. set_frame_ memory(image, 0, 0) is then called to send the image to the memory banks with 0, 0 acting as coordinates. The final command is display_ frame(), which pushes the image from memory to the display.

After the image is pushed to the display, a delay is called with delay_ ms(2000). It's expressed in milliseconds, so the 2000 means 2 seconds. The delay's purpose is essentially to set the refresh rate for the display, meaning that every 2 seconds the code will update the image by refreshing itself so that any changes enacted will be pushed to the display.

The next line begins this refresh process by calling epd.init(ped. lut_partial_update), which runs a partial update to the display. This happens to subtly refresh the pixels, unlike the rapid flashing of black and white that occurs with the full update called at the beginning of the script. This line sets the stage for a new image to be defined and then called with image.open('monocolor.bmp'), which opens the bitmap file that we've seen in the folder. By calling image.open, you can import image files that are in formats supported by PIL.

The next four lines, as shown in Figure 10-10, are what send the bitmap to the display and cause the transition during the demo code from the text and shapes to the bitmap file.

```
    # for partial update
    epd.init(epd.lut_partial_update)
    image = Image.open('monocolor.bmp')
##
 # there are 2 memory areas embedded in the e-paper display
 # and once the display is refreshed, the memory area will be auto-toggled,
 # i.e. the next action of SetFrameMemory will set the other memory area
 # therefore you have to set the frame memory twice.
 ##
    epd.set_frame_memory(image, 0, 0)
    epd.display_frame()
    epd.set_frame_memory(image, 0, 0)
    epd.display_frame()
```

Figure 10-10. *The* set_frame_memory() *commands after a new image is created*

This time, set_frame_memory(image, 0, 0), with image referring to the newly imported bitmap, and display_frame() are both called twice. As mentioned previously, the EPD has two memory banks, and by calling both of those commands twice, we make sure each bank receives the new image to display and updates. If both of these were only called once, it would cause the display to be glitchy; and if they weren't called at all, the display would not update. We didn't need to call them twice when the original image was sent, because the memory had been fully cleared using clear_frame_memory.

The final portion of the code is possibly formatted incorrectly, depending on the intent of the developer. As you can see in Figure 10-11, an additional new image is created, this time called time_image. After the parameters for this new image are set, we enter a loop using while True: that will display a rectangle with some text meant for time_image. The text is formatted to be a digital clock using time.strftime('%M:%S'). Using strftime() from the time library allows you to display real-time time data, such as a date, or in this case a clock, using custom formatting with % signs and letters, as shown with ('%M:%S'). We'll discuss this concept further when we write the code for our project.

Because we placed the time.strftime() in the loop, it will update rather than remaining static as it would when called outside the loop.

However, as discussed, for the EPD to display an updated image, both memory banks need to be reset. Because that is absent from the loop, the clock will not display, even though display_frame() is called. Instead, as you see when running the demo code, the bitmap image remains statically on the display.

It's possible that it was intended to show that you could utilize the EPD as a clock display, but the developers also wanted to keep the bitmap displayed for the purposes of the demo code. It's just important to note that if you were to set up a clock display, you would need to refresh the memory inside of the loop.

After going through the demo code, you should now have a better understanding of how the EPD works from a hardware and software perspective. There are quite a few steps to program a fully functional e-Paper display, but luckily with the various libraries and examples we're well on our way to creating our own version. With that foundation, let's move on to laying the groundwork for our project, which will involve drawing our own display image from scratch and displaying information that updates in real time, including the weather forecast using the pyowm library.

OpenWeatherMap and pyowm

Now that we're acquainted with the EPD's library and coding architecture, we can look at the pyowm coding library. pyowm is the Python wrapper for OpenWeatherMap (OWM), which is a weather API that provides access to weather and forecast data from around the world. OWM is accessed through its web site,[3] where you can create a free or paid account. The free account has all the features needed for this project.

With the account comes an API key, which you'll need in your Python code. You can access your API key through your OWM account settings under the API tab, as shown in Figure 10-11.

---

[3]https://openweathermap.org/

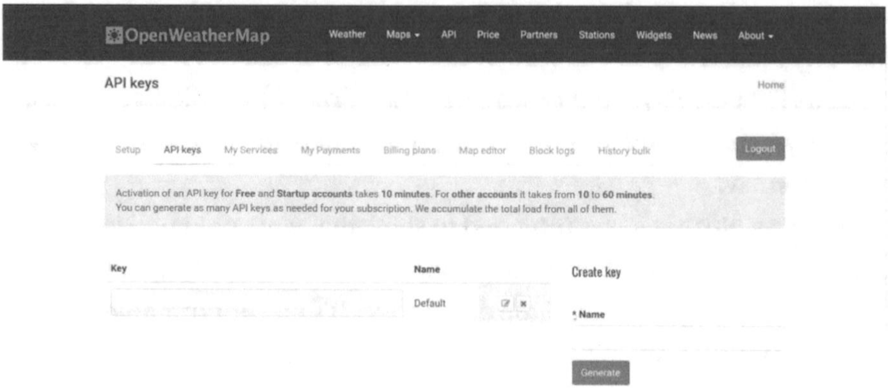

Figure 10-11. *The API tab on OWM's web site. The API key is hidden for privacy concerns. Never share your API key publicly.*

It's recommended to log in to OWM on the Tinker Board so that you can copy and paste your API key into your code instead of trying to type it, since as you'll see it's quite long and a random assortment of letters and numbers.

After you have your key, the next step will be to install the Python library on the Tinker Board. pyowm is installed using pip, so with the terminal navigate to the Home directory using cd ~ and then enter pip install pyowm.

With the library installed, you can start using it to access weather data in Python. The main process for using pyowm is to enter your API key, declare what city you want to collect data for, and then list the types of data that you want. There is an almost endless amount of data available, ranging from the broad to the detailed. The syntax for all of these functions is well documented on the pyowm project's GitHub.[4]

---

[4]https://github.com/csparpa/pyowm/blob/master/pyowm/docs/usage-examples.md

The cities are imported by including either the city name with the country code, which is a two-letter abbreviation, or the registry ID, which is a number code assigned to the city and stored in the OWM city registry, which you have access to with the library. These can be accessed in a Python script that we'll go over now and will also be available on the GitHub repo for this book.

Getting Your City ID

Start by opening a new Python file with IDLE and import the pyowm library with this statement:

```
import pyowm
```

Then, enter your API key with this:

```
owm = pyowm.OWM('api_key')
```

This means that every time owm is listed, it's referring to your API key. This way, if a feature is not available for your account level, then you won't be able to pull the data. In our case, this shouldn't be a problem.

Now we're going to call up the registry for city IDs:

```
registry = owm.city_id_registry()
```

And then create a variable called results that we'll be able to print with whichever city is looked up. We'll do that with this code:

```
results = registry.ids_for('city_name')
```

You'll be able to put any city name into the parentheses between the quotation marks. We'll then print the results to the terminal:

```
print(results)
```

Don't add quotation marks around results, because it isn't a string. We want to print the data stored in results. So, to recap, here is our complete script to gather city IDs:

```
import pyowm

owm = pyowm.OWM('api_key')

registry = owm.city_id_registry()

results = registry.ids_for('city_name')

print(results)
```

Once you enter your city's name into the parentheses as a string, run the script either in the Python shell or with TinkerOS's terminal and make note of your city ID and/or country abbreviation. You'll need it for our eventual project script. If your city is the name of a city in multiple countries, then all of them will be listed when you run the script, as shown in Figure 10-12 with Toronto, Los Angeles, and Melbourne.

```
>>>
===================== RESTART: /home/linaro/getID.py =====================
[(2800866, u'Brussels', u'BE')]
>>>
===================== RESTART: /home/linaro/getID.py =====================
[(1816670, u'Beijing', u'CN')]
>>>
===================== RESTART: /home/linaro/getID.py =====================
[(5174095, u'Toronto', u'US'), (6167865, u'Toronto', u'CA')]
>>>
===================== RESTART: /home/linaro/getID.py =====================
[(5128581, u'New York', u'US'), (5128638, u'New York', u'US')]
>>>
===================== RESTART: /home/linaro/getID.py =====================
[(1705545, u'Los Angeles', u'PH'), (3882428, u'Los Angeles', u'CL'), (5368361, u
'Los Angeles', u'US')]
>>>
===================== RESTART: /home/linaro/getID.py =====================
[(2158177, u'Melbourne', u'AU'), (2642800, u'Melbourne', u'GB'), (2642801, u'Mel
bourne', u'GB'), (4121256, u'Melbourne', u'US'), (4163971, u'Melbourne', u'US'),
 (7839805, u'Melbourne', u'AU')]
>>>
===================== RESTART: /home/linaro/getID.py =====================
[(293397, u'Tel Aviv', u'IL')]
>>> |
```

Figure 10-12. *The results of a few example cities displayed in the Python shell that were queried with our script to find city IDs*

Python Script for the Weather Display

Now that we have introduced both the EPD's Python library and the concepts behind the pyowm library, we can begin writing the code for our project. As mentioned earlier, the goal of this project is to use the EPD to display the date, time, and current weather; specifically, the temperature and current forecast. This information can be displayed in a variety of ways since the EPD is essentially a blank canvas.

For our purposes, we're going to build up a grid where the date and time will be at the top of the display and then the bottom two-thirds of the display will have four boxes. Two of them of them will be on the left side and say "Weather:" and "Temperature:" with the remaining two boxes directly across on the right side receiving the OWM data for current forecast and temperature. When everything is finished, it will look like Figure 10-13.

Figure 10-13. *The finished EPD weather display running on the Tinker Board S. You can also use the original Tinker Board as well.*

We'll begin the Python script as we have with all the others: importing library dependencies. We'll need the PIL library, the epd2in13 Python file, the time library, the math library, and of course the pyowm library. After importing these, we'll begin to declare some of these libraries' objects, beginning with epd from epd2in13.py as we saw in the demo code for the EPD. We'll also bring in the pyowm API key, specific to your account. As a result, the beginning of our code will be written like this:

```
import epd2in13
import time
from PIL import Image
from PIL import ImageDraw
from PIL import ImageFont
import pyowm
import math

epd = epd2in13.EPD()

owm = pyowm.OWM('api_key')
```

Next, we go into the main() function where we'll fully update the display as we saw in the demo code for the EPD display:

```
epd.init(epd.lut_full_update)
```

After this, we'll go into the loop. Because everything on our display will need to be updated in real time, we'll draw the image and pull the data in the loop. We'll use while True: to begin the loop and then declare objects and variables for the pyowm library.

First, we'll declare where the weather data will be collected from, with weather_at_place(), and we'll also create w = observation.get_weather(), which will be the variable to gather weather data for the pyowm library. Both will be called in the loop so that new data is constantly being gathered; otherwise, we would get the data that was originally pinged when the script was first started. The command w.get_status() is used to get the forecast. This will show things like clear, rain, clouds, snow, and so on. We're also going to print this to the console for troubleshooting purposes with `print w.get_status()`. Since `w.get_status()` outputs a string, it doesn't need to be modified when used with `print`.

Note   If you want to use the city ID number instead, you'll use `weather_at_id()` rather than `weather_at_place()`

Next, we're going to take care of the temperature data. First, we'll call `w.get_temperature('fahrenheit')['temp']`, which is the temperature equivalent to `get_status()`, but with a twist. By putting `fahrenheit` in the parentheses, the temperature will be read in Fahrenheit, however you can also use Celsius (or even Kelvin), which of course is much more common around the world.

`get_temperature()` returns a dictionary of temperature data and for our purposes we only need the current temperature, which is cataloged as `['temp']`, which is why it's being called next to `get_temperature()`. The other issue with `['temp']` is that it has a decimal attached to it, which for the display we'll want to cut off to show just the base temperature.

To parse this piece of data separately, we're going to use the `math` library that we imported earlier to use `math.trunc`. This completely cuts off the decimal of any number, leaving us with just the whole number; which in this case is the temperature.

The only remaining issue is that `math.trunc` creates an integer, which can't be printed with the `PIL draw.text()` function; it requires a string. Luckily, Python has an easy way to convert an `int` to a string, by placing `str` next to the `int` inside parentheses. We're going to create a new variable called `temp` to hold the string output for this. Finally, for troubleshooting purposes, we'll also print this data to the terminal with `print temp`. Altogether, the code will look like this:

```
while True:
        observation = owm.weather_at_place('New York,US')

        w = observation.get_weather()

        w.get_status()
        print w.get_status()

        w.get_temperature('fahrenheit')['temp']
        temp = str(math.trunc(w.get_temperature('fahrenheit')
        ['temp']))
        print temp
```

After the data, we go into the portion of the code where we draw
the image. First, much as in the demo script, we're going to declare a
new image object. However, one difference this time is that we're going
to change the width and height parameters so that the width will be
250 pixels with a height of 128 pixels. This way we can use the display
horizontally instead of vertically. We'll then bring in the draw object and
font objects as before. A change for the fonts, though, is that we'll be using
three different fonts: FreeSans, FreeSansBold and FreeSansBoldOblique.
We'll create a new font object for each and name them font, font2, and
font3. These lines will be written as follows:

```
image = Image.new('1', (250, 128), 255)
draw = ImageDraw.Draw(image)
font = ImageFont.truetype('/usr/share/fonts/
        truetype/freefont/FreeSans.ttf', 24)
font2 = ImageFont.truetype('/usr/share/fonts/
        truetype/freefont/FreeSansBold.ttf', 24)
font3 = ImageFont.truetype('/usr/share/fonts/
        truetype/freefont/FreeSansBoldOblique.
        ttf', 18)
```

Next, we'll draw our first item, a rectangle, to give a slight border around the display:

```
draw.rectangle((0, 0, 250, 128), fill = 255)
```

The rectangle will be followed by our first text items: the date and time. To do this, we'll use the `time.strftime()` function to grab this data in real time. The other aspect of these text entries is the location on the EPD. As discussed, we want these two items to be at the top of the screen and also to be in line with each other. The easiest way to think of this is to see the X axis parameter as asking "how many pixels away from the left side of the screen do you want it to be?" and the Y axis parameter as "how many pixels down from the top of the screen do you want it to be?" This will take some experimentation, since it will all be affected by the font, font size, and length of the string.

For the date, we'll enter

```
draw.text((7, 5), time.strftime('%a. %b. %d, %Y'),
font = font3, fill = 0)
```

For `time.strftime('%a. %b. %d, %Y')`, the % followed by letters all express different date parameters. In this example, %a will give us the abbreviation for the day of the week, %b will display the abbreviation for the month, %d will give us the number date and %Y will give us the year with the century number. Capitalization does count with this syntax, and you can find more information on all the items available in the `time` library's documentation.[5]

The line for the time, which will basically be a digital clock, will have a similar format to the date:

```
draw.text((170, 5), time.strftime('%l:%M%p'),
font = font3, fill = 0)
```

---

[5]https://docs.python.org/3/library/time.html

Just as with the date, `time.strftime()` is used again for the clock, but with different parameters. Here %l is used for the hour, followed by : and then %M is used for the minutes, and %p gives us either AM or PM. Just as with the date, there are more parameters available that are applicable to time-keeping.

For the coordinates, notice that the Y coordinate is the same for both the date and time. This allows them to be lined up with each other.

Now we're going to draw the first lines of our grid: first a line underneath the date and time and then a second line dividing the spaces for the date and time. To do this, we'll write

```
draw.line((250, 25, 0, 25), fill = 0)
draw.line((170, 0, 164, 25), fill = 0)
```

For the lines, there are two sets of X and Y coordinates. To make it easier to visualize, think of it as finding two points on the display and then drawing the line between them. The first line we draw is going all the way across horizontally below the date and time. The second line is a bit different because it isn't straight, it's slanted; resulting in different X values for each coordinate. This is to match the fact that the font we've chosen is italicized. The value 25 is used as the second Y coordinate so that it lines up with the horizontal line.

With that part of the image complete, we're going to move on to the forecast and temperature entries. For the forecast we want to display `"Weather:"` with the output of `get_status()` from pyowm next to it. We'll do this with the following lines:

```
draw.text((30, 35), 'Weather:', font = font2, fill = 0)
draw.text((170, 35), w.get_status(), font = font, fill = 0)
```

You'll notice that the Y coordinate is the same for both entries, just as with our date and time data, so that they'll be lined up. There's also some space allowed below the previously drawn horizontal line. By calling `w.get_status()` as the string, we make sure the forecast data output will be constantly updated.

After the forecast is the temperature, where we'll be displaying "Temperature:" followed by the current temperature data. To do this, we'll need two draw.text() entries:

```
draw.text((5, 85), 'Temperature:', font = font2, fill = 0)
draw.text((182, 85), temp + chr(176) + 'F', font = font, fill = 0)
```

Much like the way we used w.get_status() for the current forecast, we're doing a similar thing for temperature, where we're using the temp variable that we wrote earlier to hold the get_temperature() function, which has been broken down to just show the ['temp'] category without the decimal point as a string.

Additionally, this line holds the degree sign and "F" for Fahrenheit. The degree sign is obviously not freely available on a standard keyboard, so instead we're using Unicode to insert it using chr(176), which is the Unicode character number for the degree sign. The °F is placed next to the temperature data, so that it will always be directly to the right of the temperature, whether it is a single-digit or triple-digit (yikes!) number. Both lines are placed at the same Y coordinate.

Finally, to complete our image, we're going to draw two more lines, one to divide the text from the data and one to divide the forecast section from the temperature section:

```
draw.line((250, 70, 0, 70), fill = 0)
draw.line((164, 25, 164, 128), fill = 0)
```

The horizontal line crosses directly between the temperature and forecast sections, and the vertical line begins at the same coordinate (25y) as the first horizontal line so that it looks like they're crossing. This vertical line is straight, unlike the first vertical line, which was diagonal, and crosses the second horizontal line. These lines complete our image so that we can move on to writing it to the memory banks of the EPD hat.

The Technical Parts of the Script

This portion of our code will resemble the demo script, since we'll have to follow the same process of clearing and writing to the memory. First, we'll clear the memory and then set the frame memory, followed by a call to display the image. A difference is with the set_frame_memory() function. Because we're rotating the display to use it horizontally, we need to transpose the image by 270 degrees. As a result, these three lines will be written as:

```
epd.clear_frame_memory(0xFF)
epd.set_frame_memory(image.transpose(Image.ROTATE_270), 0, 0)
epd.display_frame()
```

Next, we'll add our 2-second delay, followed by a partial display update:

```
epd.delay_ms(2000)
epd.init(epd.lut_partial_update)
```

And finally, we'll reset both memory banks to fully write our updated image with our constantly updating data:

```
epd.set_frame_memory(image.transpose(Image.ROTATE_270), 0, 0)
epd.display_frame()
epd.set_frame_memory(image.transpose(Image.ROTATE_270), 0, 0)
epd.display_frame()
```

Putting that together, our final code with all the bells and whistles will look like this:

```
#!/usr/bin/env python

import epd2in13
import time
from PIL import Image
from PIL import ImageDraw
from PIL import ImageFont
```

```python
import pyowm
import math

epd = epd2in13.EPD()
owm = pyowm.OWM('insert_API_key_here')

def main():

    epd.init(epd.lut_full_update)

    while (True):

        observation = owm.weather_at_place('New York,US')
        w = observation.get_weather()
        print w.get_status() #  print forecast status
        w.get_temperature('fahrenheit')['temp']
        temp = str(math.trunc(w.get_temperature('fahrenheit')
        ['temp']))
        print w.get_temperature('fahrenheit')

        image = Image.new('1', (250, 128), 255)
        draw = ImageDraw.Draw(image)
        font = ImageFont.truetype('/usr/share/fonts/truetype/
                freefont/FreeSans.ttf', 24)
        font2 = ImageFont.truetype('/usr/share/fonts/truetype/
                freefont/FreeSansBold.ttf', 24)
        font3 = ImageFont.truetype('/usr/share/fonts/truetype/
                freefont/FreeSansBoldOblique.ttf', 18)
        draw.rectangle((0, 0, 250, 128), fill = 255)
        draw.text((7, 5), time.strftime('%a. %b. %d, %Y'),
        font = font3, fill = 0)
        draw.text((170, 5), time.strftime('%l:%M%p'),
        font = font3, fill = 0)
        draw.line((250, 25, 0, 25), fill = 0)
        draw.line((170, 0, 164, 25), fill = 0)
```

```
        draw.text((30, 35), 'Weather:', font= font2, fill = 0)
        draw.text((170, 35), w.get_status(), font = font, fill = 0)
        draw.text((5, 85), 'Temperature:', font = font2, fill = 0)
        draw.text((182, 85), temp + chr(176) + 'F', font = font,
        fill = 0)

        draw.line((164, 25, 164, 128), fill = 0)
        draw.line((250, 70, 0, 70), fill = 0)

        epd.clear_frame_memory(0xFF)
epd.set_frame_memory(image.transpose(Image.ROTATE_270), 0, 0)
        epd.display_frame()
        epd.delay_ms(2000)
        epd.init(epd.lut_partial_update)

epd.set_frame_memory(image.transpose(Image.ROTATE_270), 0, 0)
        epd.display_frame()
epd.set_frame_memory(image.transpose(Image.ROTATE_270), 0, 0)
        epd.display_frame()

if __name__ == '__main__':
    main()
```

Although the commands are fairly straightforward for displaying to the EPD, getting the placement and sizing just right can take a lot of experimentation and as a result time. However, you truly have a blank canvas to fully customize your project and have it do exactly what you want. There's just one more step to take this project to the next level...

Autorun Setup

Now that our code is written and working, we're going to configure it to run automatically when the Tinker Board boots up. This way, you can run this project without having to attach a keyboard, mouse, or display. It can be a standalone Internet-connected device, commonly referred to as headless.

However, the fact that it requires an Internet connection does mean that some special considerations must be made when setting this up. The code will not execute without an active connection, because of the pyowm library for our weather data, so it needs to be configured to execute only after the Tinker Board has booted up and there is also an active network connection present.

To do this, we'll set up our Python script to be executable, so that it can launch on its own. Then we'll place the script and its dependencies into a folder found under /etc/network called if-up.d. This folder contains scripts that automatically run once a network connection is established (thus the naming convention "if-up"). The only caveat here is that this folder requires root access. Files cannot simply be dragged and dropped into it. For that reason, we'll be doing this work through the terminal.

Note   Although everything is being done through the terminal, it's recommended to have the GUI file directory open to the if-up.d folder to double-check that everything is working properly.

First, we'll make our Python script an executable file. We went over this process briefly in the GPIO chapter while discussing the ways to run our Python code. We need to add the following line to the top of our script:

```
#!/usr/bin/env python
```

Save your script and then open a terminal, changing directories to your project's folder, and enter chmod a+x weatherDisplay.py. Nothing will seem to happen in the terminal, but if you click the file in the GUI, you'll be given the choice to run the script without any other commands. You can also run it via the terminal with sudo ./weatherDisplay.py.

Speaking of our script's name, we need to remove the `.py` extension for this method to work properly. We can do this easily in the GUI by right-clicking the file and renaming it. We need to do this because any files that have an extension like that will not run in the `if-up.d` folder.

Now that the prep work is taken care of, we can begin the process of moving everything to the `if-up.d` folder. As mentioned previously, this folder is only accessible as root. To use the terminal as `root` enter `sudo su`. This automatically brings you back to the Home directory by default. You'll be able to confirm that you are `root` by checking the terminal, which should show `root@tinkerboard`, as in Figure 10-14.

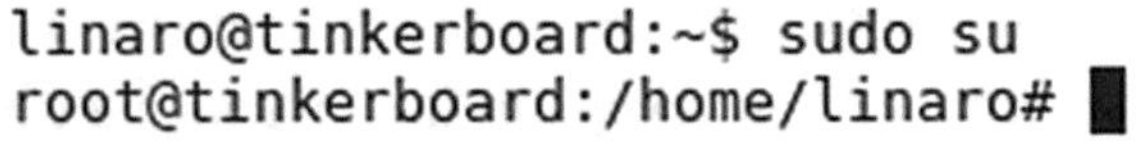

```
linaro@tinkerboard:~$ sudo su
root@tinkerboard:/home/linaro# █
```

Figure 10-14. *`root@tinkerboard` in the terminal*

As `root`, change directories to the `if-up.d` folder with `cd /etc/network/if-up.d`. Again, it's recommended to double-check your work by having the file directory GUI opened to the same `if-up.d` folder. Now we're going to copy the project folder, which for the purposes of this example will be called `projectFolder`. The `projectFolder` will need to contain the script and library dependencies. We'll copy it into the `if-up.d` folder using the following terminal command

```
cp -r /home/linaro/projectFolder /etc/network/if-up.d.
```

Note   You may need to place copies of the Python libraries, including pyowm, into the `projectFolder` depending on how you've set up Python and `pip` directories on your Tinker Board. It will also depend on how future iterations of TinkerOS and the kernel handle this as well.

Basically, you're using the copy command, cp, and then listing the file location of the folder you wish to copy, followed by a space, and then the file location of the folder where you want to copy your original folder to; also known as the target folder.

After executing the command, you should see your project folder appear in the if-up.d folder in the GUI. The next step is to get all the files out of the project folder and directly into the if-up.d folder. We could have copied each individual file over, but by copying the folder we can perform this task more succinctly by moving the contents of the file folder up one level in the file directory using the mv command. Enter

```
mv /etc/network/if-up.d/projectFolder/* /etc/network/if-up.d/
projectFolder/.* .
```

Note the space between the last * and . at the end of the line. By entering the file extension of the project folder with that syntax, you ensure that all folders and files are moved up a level, even if their file names begin with a period (.). Omitting the space could cause errors; especially when dealing with code library files that may use unique naming conventions. After executing the command, you should see all the files and folders from the project folder appear directly into the if-up.d folder.

Everything should be ready to go, but first we need to clean things up a bit. The project folder is empty now and is no longer necessary, so we should remove it. We'll do that using the rm (remove) command. This is a very powerful command; once you execute it, it will immediately remove the targeted file or folder, so always be cautious when using it.

The rm command has different flags for whether you are deleting a single file or an entire folder. The flag for a folder, or directory, is -r. Also, instead of typing out the entire file directory location, you'll only include the name of the folder you're removing. So, the command to remove the now empty project folder inside if-up.d is rm -r projectFolder. You should see the folder disappear from the file directory GUI.

Before we reboot to see if our script starts up correctly with a network connection, we should test to make sure the script can run properly from the if-up.d folder. Run the script in the terminal using ./weatherDisplay (no sudo is needed, since we're still root) to make sure that no errors appear. If you get any missing dependency errors, then you'll need to copy those library folders, as mentioned previously in the note, over to the if-up.d folder. You can use the same cp process for this that we went over earlier.

If the EPD displays as expected, then it's time to reboot the Tinker Board using reboot. If all goes as planned, then after TinkerOS boots to the desktop with a successful network connection you should see the EPD begin the script by doing the full update and then updating the date, time, and weather in real time.

Finishing Touches

With all the coding and Linux work done, you have a fully functional Internet-connected information display. Because it is headless, you can place it anywhere with a connection to power, and have it run. There are some aesthetic things you can do, though, to bring it to the next level.

Instead of simply leaving the Tinker Board with the EPD display exposed to the elements, you can put it in a housing of some sort. As we discussed in the first chapter, there are a variety of cases available that will fit the Tinker Board's form factor. Many of these cases have openings to allow access to the GPIO pins and as a result, the Tinker Board could be protected from environmental and physical hazards while having the EPD display remain attached and unaffected by the housing.

There are also fully DIY options out there with the only limitation being your imagination. There's always the option of 3D printing or milling a custom case. Another popular option for EPD projects is to utilize a picture frame, or similarly functional household item, to allow the display to blend in with its surroundings in a home.

Of course, you aren't just limited to showing the data parameters that we coded for in this project. These displays can basically show any information that you want. There are many calendar, news, and social media APIs available for Python that you can utilize in your code to fully customize the kind of EPD project that you want. You can also animate these displays further with the PIL library and integrate them with larger projects.

This chapter has shown how you can integrate programming with the Tinker Board to create fully customized projects and given you the tools to go further with your own ideas; which has truly been the goal of this entire book. We have one more project in front of us, and it is a classic: a robot!

CHAPTER 11

Project 5: Build a Robot with a Streaming Camera Feed

It's been a long journey, but we've reached our final project in this book. The previous four projects focused on practical uses for the Tinker Board, but for the grand finale we're going to stray a bit from the practical and build a simple robot that can be operated via a custom Bluetooth controller and will stream video.

Why a Robot?

A robot is the quintessential electronics project. Robots come in many varieties and can be very simple or incredibly complex. By now you're well aware of the Tinker Board's features, and once again the Internet connectivity, full operating system, and diverse IO options beyond GPIO make it a great platform for a robot with more features than your average beginner robot.

© Liz Clark 2019
L. Clark, *Practical Tinker Board*, https://doi.org/10.1007/978-1-4842-3826-4_11

Robot Supplies

For the construction of the robot, we'll be using two DC motors with wheels attached to a mini robot chassis. If you want to use a different motor type, such as gearbox motors, you can. The concept will be the same. For the chassis, there are countless options available on the market, and the one you choose really comes down to personal preference since its purpose is to hold the electronics and attach the motors. Different shapes, colors, or materials won't affect the robot's technical outcome.

To keep everything mobile, the Tinker Board will be powered by a USB battery bank, which will be mounted to whatever chassis you choose. You'll need a high-capacity battery bank, especially with the Tinker Board's amperage concerns. Luckily, these larger capacity battery banks are becoming more common and are also available in smaller sizes. Because of this you will probably get better power results with the original Tinker Board than the Tinker Board S, since the Tinker Board S needs 3A to boot.

Of course, something needs to control the motors, since hardware PWM is not available on the Tinker Board's GPIO and is a necessary feature when it comes to controlling motors. As a result, we'll be using another HAT, this time by Adafruit, specifically the Motor HAT. Additionally, we'll use their Python library for the HAT, which will make coding the motors' movement a lot more straightforward.

Adafruit was mentioned in the GPIO chapter as an option for procuring electronics supplies. In addition to selling standard electronics components, they're also an open source hardware company in the United States that designs, manufactures, and supports a variety of boards produced in-house.

I2C

The HAT communicates with the Tinker Board through I2C (Inter-integrated Circuit, pronounced "I squared C"), which is a serial communication protocol that is very similar to SPI in that it allows for multiple integrated circuits to communicate with each other. However, I2C requires only two pins to communicate with multiple devices; by contrast, SPI requires four pins for each connected device and a dedicated IO pin from the master device for each connected device. I2C-connected devices are also a bit easier to manage and don't require as much setup as SPI.

The HAT has onboard electronics, including PWM drivers, terminal connectors for motors, and a dedicated power input for the motors, which receive I2C communication that then control the motors and anything else attached to the pins, as shown in Figure 11-1.

Figure 11-1. *The Adafruit Motor HAT*

Robot Extras

To give our robot some extra flair, we're going to implement a camera into its design. We'll use either a webcam or a camera module connected to the CSI connector on the Tinker Board, like the one we used in the Android chapter, to stream a video feed to a webpage on your network while we drive the robot around. We'll be able to mount the camera to the front of the robot chassis and have it act almost like the robot's eyes.

Speaking of driving around, we'll need to control the robot, and this creates a great opportunity to build a custom controller that communicates via Bluetooth. To do that we'll use an additional Adafruit development board that's Arduino-compatible (meaning that you can code it using the Arduino IDE and Arduino code libraries), called the 32u4 Bluetooth Feather.

But if you don't want to build a custom controller, you don't have to. We'll be controlling the robot with keyboard inputs, so our custom controller will be a macro keyboard in disguise. As a result, you can use the same wireless or Bluetooth keyboard you've been using the whole time with your Tinker Board.

This entire project will again take place in TinkerOS. So, let's begin by booting into TinkerOS and setting up the Python library for the HAT.

Motor HAT Setup

Let's begin the setup for the Motor HAT by following the steps outlined by Adafruit to install the Python library.[1] First, we'll need to change directories to the Home directory and install the dependencies, most of which should already be installed if you've been following along with the other chapters.

Navigate to a terminal and enter

```
sudo apt-get install build-essential python-dev python-smbus
```

Then, as we've done before, we're going to clone into the GitHub repo with

```
git clone https://github.com/adafruit/Adafruit-Motor-HAT-
Python-Library.git
```

---

[1]https://learn.adafruit.com/adafruit-dc-and-stepper-motor-hat-for-raspberry-pi/installing-software

After that finishes, change directories into the newly cloned folder with `cd ~/Adafruit-Motor-HAT-Python-Library`. Once in the folder, we have a Python setup script to run. In the terminal, type `sudo python setup.py install`.

After you've run the `setup.py` script, the library is ready to use. Adafruit provides some example code in the examples folder along with the `Robot.py` file, which has the main components of the library, as shown in Figure 11-2.

```
                                              Robot.py - /ho

File  Edit  Format  Run  Options  Window  Help

class Robot(object):
    def __init__(self, addr=0x60, left_id=1, right_id=2, left_trim=0, right_trim=0,
                 stop_at_exit=True):
        """Create an instance of the robot.  Can specify the following optional
        parameters:
         - addr: The I2C address of the motor HAT, default is 0x60.
         - left_id: The ID of the left motor, default is 1.
         - right_id: The ID of the right motor, default is 2.
         - left_trim: Amount to offset the speed of the left motor, can be positive
                      or negative and use useful for matching the speed of both
                      motors.  Default is 0.
         - right_trim: Amount to offset the speed of the right motor (see above).
         - stop_at_exit: Boolean to indicate if the motors should stop on program
                         exit.  Default is True (highly recommended to keep this
                         value to prevent damage to the bot on program crash!).
        """
        # Initialize motor HAT and left, right motor.
        self._mh = Adafruit_MotorHAT(addr)
        self._left = self._mh.getMotor(left_id)
        self._right = self._mh.getMotor(right_id)
        self._left_trim = left_trim
        self._right_trim = right_trim
        # Start with motors turned off.
        self._left.run(Adafruit_MotorHAT.RELEASE)
        self._right.run(Adafruit_MotorHAT.RELEASE)
        # Configure all motors to stop at program exit if desired.
        if stop_at_exit:
            atexit.register(self.stop)

    def _left_speed(self, speed):
        """Set the speed of the left motor, taking into account its trim offset.
        """
        assert 0 <= speed <= 255, 'Speed must be a value between 0 to 255 inclusive!'
        speed += self._left_trim
        speed = max(0, min(255, speed))  # Constrain speed to 0-255 after trimming.
        self._left.setSpeed(speed)

    def _right_speed(self, speed):
        """Set the speed of the right motor, taking into account its trim offset.
        """
        assert 0 <= speed <= 255, 'Speed must be a value between 0 to 255 inclusive!'
        speed += self._right_trim
        speed = max(0, min(255, speed))  # Constrain speed to 0-255 after trimming.
        self._right.setSpeed(speed)

    def stop(self):
        """Stop all movement."""
        self._left.run(Adafruit_MotorHAT.RELEASE)
        self._right.run(Adafruit_MotorHAT.RELEASE)

    def forward(self, speed, seconds=None):
        """Move forward at the specified speed (0-255).  Will start moving
        forward and return unless a seconds value is specified, in which
        case the robot will move forward for that amount of time and then stop.
        """
        # Set motor speed and move both forward.
        self._left_speed(speed)
        self._right_speed(speed)
        self._left.run(Adafruit_MotorHAT.FORWARD)
        self._right.run(Adafruit_MotorHAT.FORWARD)
        # If an amount of time is specified, move for that time and then stop.
        if seconds is not None:
            time.sleep(seconds)
            self.stop()
```

Figure 11-2. *The Robot.py library file*

The main takeaway from Robot.py is that it has functions written to define the pulses for the motors for different speeds and directions. This means that when you write your own code with Robot.py imported, you can use simple commands like robot.direction(speed, time), where you enter a direction parameter, speed parameter, and then how long you want your robot to do that action, and your robot is on the move.

As you can see in Figure 11-2, the files for this library have very detailed comments explaining what each line is doing, which you can read at your leisure if you need to clarify anything.

Connecting the Hardware

The software won't do much, though, without the hardware connected. First, we'll connect the two DC motors to the Motor HAT by plugging their power and ground wires into the terminal connectors on the HAT as shown in Figure 11-3.

Figure 11-3. *The motors connected to the terminal blocks on the Motor HAT. You'll need a small screwdriver to tighten the terminal blocks.*

Next, plug the HAT into the GPIO pins. This HAT fits over the stock heat sink, but just barely. For robots planned to rack up a lot of miles and as a result give off more heat, you may want to consider a riser header like the one we used in the last chapter for the EPD HAT. The final step is to connect the external battery power for the motors to the HAT, as shown in Figure 11-4. AA and AAA battery boxes that have wire connections for power and ground are sold for applications like this.

Figure 11-4. *The power terminal connector for the motors on the HAT*

Running the Example Code

Once everything is connected to the Tinker Board, the demo code we're going to try is RobotTest.py. It basically has a sequence of commands to make sure everything is hooked up properly by pulsing the motors at different PWM frequencies. Each sequence is on a timer without a loop, so the script runs through once and then stops.

To run it, while still in the examples folder, enter sudo python RobotTest.py into the terminal. Your motors should start spinning for a few seconds each at different speeds. If you run it with your robot fully assembled, you'll also see that it's going backward, forward, left, and right.

If we look at the code, by entering idle RobotTest.py into the terminal, we can see the syntax that's making this script tick, or rather pulse. As you can see in Figure 11-5, the code begins by importing Robot and then setting up the motors with calls to the imported Robot.py file.

```
RobotTest.py - /h

File  Edit  Format  Run  Options  Window  Help

# Simple two DC motor robot class usage example.
# Author: Tony DiCola
# License: MIT License https://opensource.org/licenses/MIT
import time

# Import the Robot.py file (must be in the same directory as this file!).
import Robot


# Set the trim offset for each motor (left and right).  This is a value that
# will offset the speed of movement of each motor in order to make them both
# move at the same desired speed.  Because there's no feedback the robot doesn't
# know how fast each motor is spinning and the robot can pull to a side if one
# motor spins faster than the other motor.  To determine the trim values move the
# robot forward slowly (around 100 speed) and watch if it veers to the left or
# right.  If it veers left then the _right_ motor is spinning faster so try
# setting RIGHT_TRIM to a small negative value, like -5, to slow down the right
# motor.  Likewise if it veers right then adjust the _left_ motor trim to a small
# negative value.  Increase or decrease the trim value until the bot moves
# straight forward/backward.
LEFT_TRIM  = 0
RIGHT_TRIM = 0


# Create an instance of the robot with the specified trim values.
# Not shown are other optional parameters:
#  - addr: The I2C address of the motor HAT, default is 0x60.
#  - left_id: The ID of the left motor, default is 1.
#  - right_id: The ID of the right motor, default is 2.
robot = Robot.Robot(left_trim=LEFT_TRIM, right_trim=RIGHT_TRIM)

# Now move the robot around!
# Each call below takes two parameters:
#  - speed: The speed of the movement, a value from 0-255.  The higher the value
#           the faster the movement.  You need to start with a value around 100
#           to get enough torque to move the robot.
#  - time (seconds):  Amount of time to perform the movement.  After moving for
#                     this amount of seconds the robot will stop.  This parameter
#                     is optional and if not specified the robot will start moving
#                     forever.
robot.forward(150, 1.0)    # Move forward at speed 150 for 1 second.
robot.left(200, 0.5)       # Spin left at speed 200 for 0.5 seconds.
robot.forward(150, 1.0)    # Repeat the same movement 3 times below...
robot.left(200, 0.5)
robot.forward(150, 1.0)
robot.left(200, 0.5)
robot.forward(150, 1.0)
robot.right(200, 0.5)

# Spin in place slowly for a few seconds.
robot.right(100)  # No time is specified so the robot will start spinning forever.
time.sleep(2.0)   # Pause for a few seconds while the robot spins (you could do
                  # other processing here though!).
robot.stop()      # Stop the robot from moving.

# Now move backwards and spin right a few times.
robot.backward(150, 1.0)
robot.right(200, 0.5)
robot.backward(150, 1.0)
robot.right(200, 0.5)
robot.backward(150, 1.0)
robot.right(200, 0.5)
robot.backward(150, 1.0)

# That's it!  Note that on exit the robot will automatically stop moving.
```

Figure 11-5. *The RobotTest.py file*

Then we can see how the different motor movements are called using the same syntax that we discussed earlier: `robot.direction(speed, time)`. That's basically the entire script. The `Robot.py` library file makes it very simple to program in motor movements. Let's move on now to starting our robot project code.

Robot Project Python Code

When you're beginning to write code for any project, it's important to break the process down into the basic goals that you want to accomplish, as we did when planning the EPD project in Chapter 10. In its most basic form, we want our robot to be able to go forward, backward, left, and right and to stop. Each of these directions will be controlled with a button, which points us in the direction of using `if` statements; for example, "if this button is pressed, have the robot do this."

To implement these controls, we're going to use keyboard inputs. This way, you can either use your attached keyboard or build the upcoming custom Bluetooth controller, which will send the same keyboard commands. The camera portion of the project will be separate from the Python code. With everything planned, we can start writing our code.

In Python, you can have keyboard inputs affect code execution by using the `readchar` library. It's installed using `pip`, so you'll need to change directories to the Home folder and enter `pip install readchar` into the terminal to install.

After the installation, change directories back to the Motor HAT's examples folder and open IDLE to create a new file. First, we'll import our dependencies: `time`, `Robot`, and `readchar`. Robot is, of course, the Adafruit library file, which we will need to keep in the same folder as the project file, just as we experienced with the EPD project and the Waveshare dependencies. Those first three lines will look like this:

```
import time
import Robot
import readchar
```

Then, we'll set up the needed items for the Robot library, just like the code we saw in RobotTest.py, with these lines:

```
LEFT_TRIM = 0
RIGHT_TRIM = 0
Robot = Robot.Robot(left_trim=LEFT_TRIM, right_trim=RIGHT_TRIM)
```

After that, we'll go right into the loop. We'll be setting everything up for readchar in the loop rather than outside it. The syntax for readchar is to first set up a variable that is equal to readchar.readkey(), so that we can plug in any of various keyboard inputs and have the readchar library know it should interpret that as keyboard input. We do that with this line:

```
key = readchar.readkey()
```

The keys that we'll be using are W, A, S, D and B. The WASD keys were chosen since they're traditionally used for movement controls in PC gaming. W controls forward movement, A for left, D for right and S for backward movement. B will be used for stopping, as B stands for brake. As discussed before, we'll be using if statements to integrate our keyboard inputs with our motor movements. The syntax will be this:

```
if (key == 'w'):
        robot.forward(150)
        print('forward\n')
        time.sleep(0.1)
```

To break that if statement down, if W is pressed, then the robot will move forward at 75% speed. The string forward will also be printed to the terminal for troubleshooting purposes and there will be a slight delay to keep everything running smoothly. Since the script is going to be waiting for keystrokes, the delay will avoid any lag or scenario of commands running into each other in an infinite loop. If the delay is set to be too long, however, you will experience a noticeable lag.

Note   An important point about the `readchar` library is that anything that you put in the (`key` == `' '`) parentheses is case-sensitive. As result, if you want just a simple keystroke to be read, be sure to keep the enclosed letters lowercase.

Using exactly the same formatting, we'll now create `if` statements for the other key inputs. But because we want to allow different inputs, the rest of the statements will be `elif` statements, Python's syntax for `else-if`. The rest of the key inputs will look like this:

```
elif (key == 'a'):
        robot.left(150)
        print('left\n')
        time.sleep(0.1)
elif (key == 's'):
        robot.backward(150)
        print('backward\n')
        time.sleep(0.1)
elif (key == 'd'):
        robot.right(150)
        print('right\n')
        time.sleep(0.1)
elif (key == 'b'):
        robot.stop()
        print('brake!\n')
        time.sleep(0.1)
```

The only big difference among the different robot movements is that robot.stop() does not include a speed parameter, since it's effectively taking away all speed. The entire script will look like this:

```
import time
import Robot
import readchar

LEFT_TRIM = 0
RIGHT_TRIM = 0
robot = Robot.Robot(left_trim=LEFT_TRIM, right_trim=RIGHT_TRIM)

while True:
    key = readchar.readkey()

    if (key == 'w'):
        robot.forward(150)
        print('forward\n')
        time.sleep(0.1)
    elif (key == 'a'):
        robot.left(150)
        print('left\n')
        time.sleep(0.1)
    elif (key == 's'):
        robot.backward(150)
        print('backward\n')
        time.sleep(0.1)
    elif (key == 'd'):
        robot.right(150)
        print('right\n')
        time.sleep(0.1)
    elif (key == 'b'):
        robot.stop()
        print('brake!\n')
        time.sleep(0.1)
```

It's a relatively short script, thanks to the Robot.py library. Now you can save this as roboTinker.py and test it via the terminal with sudo python roboTinker.py. Using your attached keyboard (wireless of course), you should be able to control the motors and see confirmation in the terminal that you're sending the correct commands as shown in Figure 11-6.

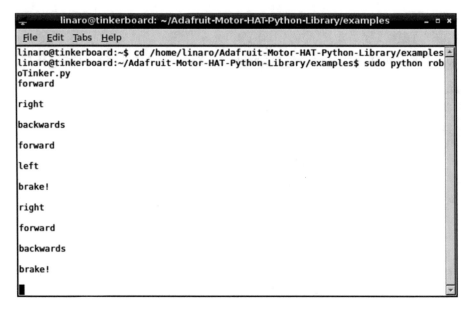

Figure 11-6. *The confirmation strings that the* roboTinker *script has received the keyboard inputs for control*

Configuring the Camera

We're going to take a break from the Motor HAT for a moment and work on the camera portion of this project. We'll be using a camera, either a USB webcam or a ribbon cable camera, as essentially a set of eyes for the robot to navigate with.

The camera feed will be streamed with a piece of software called MJPG-streamer, which allows you to receive a video feed from a device on your network, in this case the Tinker Board, via a browser. You'll have to be on another device on the same network to receive the stream, but it should at least allow you to explore your home without leaving the couch.

Webcam vs. Ribbon Cable Camera

You can use MJPG-streamer with either a webcam or a camera module, which plugs into the MIPI connector on the Tinker Board as shown in Figure 11-7 and discussed as an Android example in Chapter 6.

Figure 11-7. *The CSI-cam connected to the Tinker Board*

There are pros and cons for each camera choice. For the webcam, you'll more than likely get better picture quality, and a USB connection is easier for hot-swapping peripherals; but it is much larger than a camera module, and you'll have to manage the longer USB cable when assembling your robot. The housing for the webcam may also create issues with mounting the camera to the robot chassis.

The camera module is a much smaller form factor than a webcam, and you can either purchase an aftermarket case for mounting it or create your own using 3D printing or CNC. The ribbon cable can be swapped for different lengths to best suit your project, and plugging directly into the top of the Tinker Board can also help to keep things tidy. However, the camera module will have a lower picture quality than a webcam and often requires a well-lit area to have the best results. The MIPI connector is also finicky on both the camera module and the Tinker Board. Additionally, the camera module is highly sensitive to static shock and should only be handled in a grounded area. The connectors and ribbon cables are also very fragile, so the entire camera must be handled with care.

As you can see, the camera type you choose will come down to your goals for the robot and personal preference. Luckily, the same software can be used for either choice, so let's move on to setting up MJPG-streamer.

Installing MJPG-streamer

MJPG-streamer is run through the terminal, so we won't be using Python or any other programming language. We will need to install some dependency programs and drivers though. Navigate to the terminal and enter

```
sudo apt-get install subversion libjpeg-dev libjpeg62-turbo-dev
imagemagick libv4l-dev uvcdynctrl
```

to install them.

After that we'll use `subversion`, which we just installed, to download MJPG-streamer from the server location where it's hosted. With the terminal, enter `svn co https://svn.code.sf.net/p/mjpg-streamer/code/` to download the folder into the Home directory.

After downloading, change directories to the new folder using `cd ~/code/mjpg-streamer`. MJPG-streamer utilizes a make file to install, so while in the directory enter make followed by `sudo make install` into the terminal. Once the installation completes, you're ready to try MJPG-streamer.

Running MJPG-streamer

To use MJPG-streamer, you of course need to connect your chosen camera device. This needs to be done while the Tinker Board is powered off, because during boot, the Tinker Board will detect that the camera is connected and create a video device under /dev; otherwise, your camera will not be recognized. Once your camera is connected, power up the Tinker Board and via the terminal change directories to the MJPG-streamer folder with `cd ~/code/mjpg-streamer`.

From the folder, we'll run the MJPG-streamer program. There are a few configurable parts for MJPG-streamer. The first is calling MJPG-streamer, with `./mjpg-streamer`. Next you select an input device and settings with `-i "./input_uvc.so -y`. Here the UVC video plug-in is initialized as the video input, and `-y` indicates that the YUYV video format will be used over MJPG.

The next few parameters are optional but have been shown to achieve smooth streaming results on the Tinker Board and avoid any errors.

- `-r` sets the resolution; and since we're streaming, a lower resolution will guarantee smooth video via the network.

- 640×480 is an option that balances between image quality and streaming quality. Of course, you can use a resolution as high as your camera supports.

- `-f` sets the frame rate, or FPS, for the video, and depending on your region and goals for the project this may vary. 30 FPS will create a very smooth picture.

- Finally, `-n` blocks the initialization of the dynamic control features (`dynctrls`) in the Linux-UVC library. This will depend on your camera and its drivers, but you have a lower chance of throwing errors if you disable it.

Combined, the entire input portion will be listed as `-i "./input_uvc.so -y -r 640x480 -f 30 -n"`.

Next is the output portion, basically how the video is being pushed to the stream on the network. It begins with `-o`, followed by `"./output_http.so` for streaming with the HTTP plug-in, followed by `-w ./www"` so that the files will be written to the web page for the stream rather than a subfolder, and as a result are not saved anywhere.

The full terminal command will be

```
./mjpg_streamer -i "input_uvc.so -y -r 640x480 -f 30 -n" -o "./
output_http.so -w ./www"
```

If executed with zero errors, this will return the output shown in Figure 11-8 via the terminal and will begin streaming over the network.

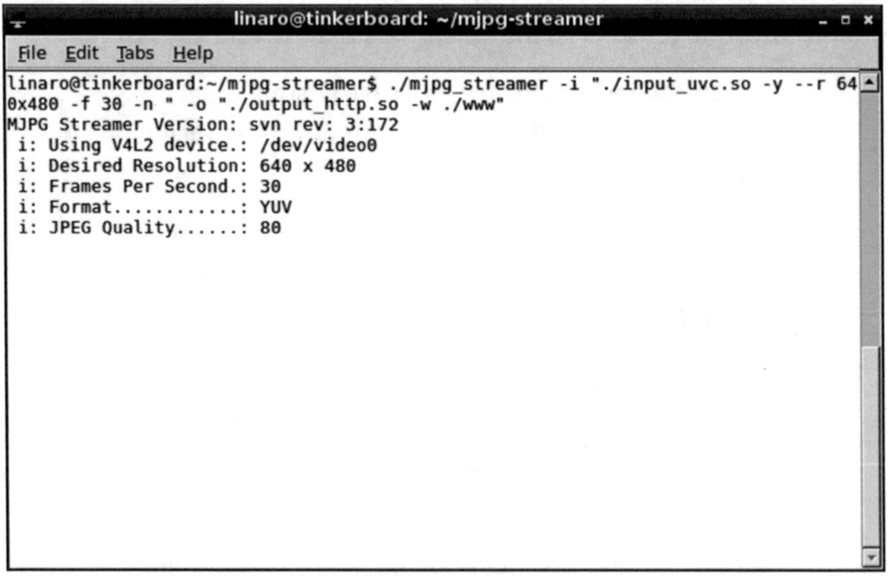

```
linaro@tinkerboard: ~/mjpg-streamer                               _ □ ✕
File  Edit  Tabs  Help
linaro@tinkerboard:~/mjpg-streamer$ ./mjpg_streamer -i "./input_uvc.so -y --r 64
0x480 -f 30 -n " -o "./output_http.so -w ./www"
MJPG Streamer Version: svn rev: 3:172
 i: Using V4L2 device.: /dev/video0
 i: Desired Resolution: 640 x 480
 i: Frames Per Second.: 30
 i: Format............: YUV
 i: JPEG Quality......: 80
```

Figure 11-8. *MJPG-streamer executed without errors via the terminal*

On a device on your network, you can enter the following URL into a browser to see the stream: `http://111.111.1.1:8080/?action=stream`, where `111.111.1.1` will be your Tinker Board's IP address, as shown in Figure 11-9. You can also view the stream on the Tinker Board in a browser with `http://127.0.0.1:8080/?action=stream`.

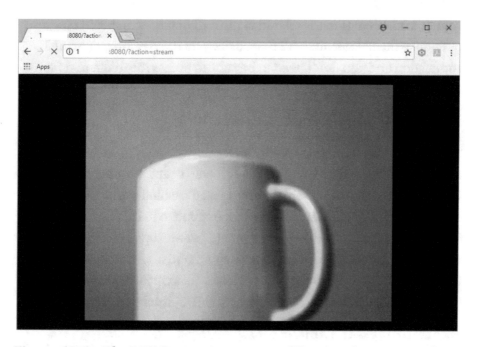

Figure 11-9. *The MJPG-streamer streamed live in a browser on the network. The camera feed seen here is from a ribbon cable camera module.*

Start on Boot

Much as we needed to have our EPD project start up on boot, we'll do the same thing with our robot so that we don't have to worry about an HDMI connection interfering with our chassis. We're going to target the same network folder, `if-up.d`, for MJPG-streamer, since it requires a network connection. MJPG-streamer is terminal-based, though, so how will we have it launch without typing into the terminal? We're going to use a type of script called a Bash script. You can put anything that you would normally type into the terminal in a Bash script to have it run as an executable file.

For our roboTinker Python script, we're going to launch it from a file called autostart, which is in the .config/lxsession/LXDE folder path. It contains other commands related to the GUI that need to begin on startup, but unlike the files located in if-up.d, they do not require a network connection and you don't need to be root to access the folder and file.

Bash Script for MJPG-Streamer

To create our Bash script for MJPG-streamer, we'll first need to create a new text file. To do this we'll enter sudo nano start_streamer.sh into the terminal. This creates and enters into a text file called start_streamer.sh. In our blank text file, we'll first enter our line to make it executable. This is similar to the line that we've entered at the top of our Python scripts previously. The technical term for this command is a *shebang*, because it begins with #!. The shebang syntax for a Bash script is #!/bin/bash.

Next, we'll define our library path for MJPG-streamer with

```
export LD_LIBRARY_PATH=/home/linaro/mjpg-streamer/
```

Finally, our last line will be similar to what we put in the terminal once inside the /mjpg-streamer directory. We'll put

```
/home/linaro/mjpg-streamer/mjpg_streamer -i "/home/linaro/mjpg-
streamer/input_uvc.so -y -r 640x480 -f 30 -n" -o "/home/linaro/
mjpg-streamer/output_http.so -w ./www"
```

The full file extensions are there for the program path and input and output plug-ins, since this won't be running directly from the file directory as it would if we were executing it from the terminal. The final Bash script will look like this:

```
#!/bin/bash
export LD_LIBRARY_PATH=/home/linaro/mjpg-streamer/

/home/linaro/mjpg-streamer/mjpg_streamer -I "/home/linaro/mjpg-
streamer/input_uvc.so -y -r 640x480 -f 30 -n" -o "/home/linaro/
mjpg-streamer/output_http.so -w ./www"
```

Once you have that in the text file, save and exit the nano editor, which will bring you back to the terminal. Now, much as we've done with Python scripts, we'll use chmod to make our Bash script executable. Enter sudo chmod +x start_streamer.sh into the terminal and then sudo ./start_streamer.sh to test. If all has gone well, MJPG-streamer should begin running.

Copying `start_streamer.sh` to `if-up.d`

After we've made start_streamer.sh an executable, we can move it to the if-up.d folder. Before we can do that, though, we need to remove the .sh file extension from the filename, because files with file extensions cannot run in the if-up.d folder. Rename the file to start_streamer via the GUI and then we can copy it over to the if-up.d folder.

To begin the copying process, just as we did with the EPD project, we need to enter the terminal as root using sudo su. Next, we'll change directories to if-up.d with cd /etc/network/if-up.d. Finally, we'll copy the start_streamer file with

```
cp -r /home/linaro/start_streamer /etc/network/if-up.d
```

Note that the file location for the file to be copied is listed first, followed by the target file location, which in this case is if-up.d.

Launching **roboTinker.py** with autostart

Previously with our EPD project, we copied our Python files into `if-up.d` so that they would run on startup once a network connection was established. However, since we're using `readchar` for inputs in our `roboTinker.py` file, it needs to run in the terminal because `readchar` does not work when executed through IDLE. As a result, we're going to use the command `lxterminal` inside the `autostart` executable to run `roboTinker.py` via a terminal window that will open upon startup and remain open to receive our `readchar` commands.

First, we'll edit the `autostart` text file by entering `sudo nano /home/linaro/.config/lxsession/LXDE/autostart` into the terminal. You'll see three lines that already exist in `autostart`. We're going to insert our line for `roboTinker.py` with

```
@lxterminal -e sudo python /home/linaro/Adafruit-Motor-HAT-
Python-Library/examples/roboTinker.py
```

into the third line space, as shown in Figure 11-10. This tells the script to open a terminal window and execute the `roboTinker.py` file. Then save the `autostart` file and return to the terminal. We're now ready to reboot to test that both MJPG-streamer and `roboTinker.py` begin automatically.

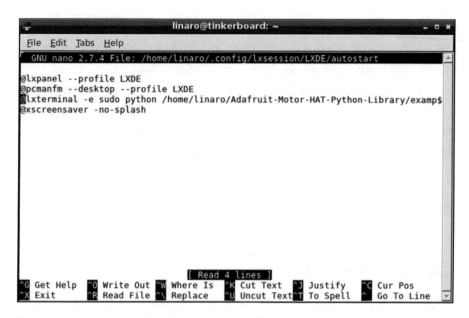

Figure 11-10. The edited autostart file

Bonus: Bluetooth Controller Coded with Arduino IDE

As a bonus project to accompany the robot, we can also build a custom controller as discussed earlier in this chapter. One of the great things about DIY electronics and maker projects is that they can have multiple components and involve as many different platforms as you want.

For our custom controller, we're going to be using a 32u4 Bluetooth Feather development board by Adafruit, the same company that made the Motor HAT we're using to control the motors for our robot. This board can be coded using the Arduino IDE, which is the official coding interface used with Arduino boards.

The 32u4 processor used on this Feather board can act as an HID device without a firmware switch when coded with the Arduino libraries for it. There is also a BLE Arduino library from Adafruit available, along

309

with example code, that we'll be able to utilize for this mini-project. We'll just add some minor edits, specifically the GPIO pins and keycodes, to the example code and then be ready to use our controller.

The example code[2] and Bluetooth Arduino library[3] are both available via Adafruit's GitHub or their Learn system web site with full instructions for setting up the Arduino IDE to use the board. The two lines we'll need to edit are the arrays for both the IO pins utilized and keycodes; revise lines 112 and 113 to look like this:

```
int inputPins[5]     = { 5          , 6          , 9
, 10         , 11         };
int inputKeycodes[5] = { HID_KEY_B, HID_KEY_D, HID_KEY_W
, HID_KEY_S, HID_KEY_A};
```

where both arrays are set to have five items. The order matters for both the digital pins and keycodes, where the first index in each array will be paired; meaning that digital pin 5 will send a keystroke for B, pin 6 will send D, and so on. This aspect of the code will all depend on how your circuit is set up.

Circuit

For the circuit, we'll use five temporary push buttons, just as we did in the GPIO chapter. One side of each button will be grounded and the other side will be routed to its appropriate IO pin on the Feather board. We'll be utilizing digital pins 5, 6, 9, 10 and 11 as shown in the circuit diagram in Figure 11-11.

---

[2]https://learn.adafruit.com/custom-wireless-bluetooth-cherry-mx-gamepad?view=all#uploading-sketch-to-adafruit-feather-ble
[3]https://learn.adafruit.com/adafruit-feather-32u4-bluefruit-le/using-with-arduino-ide

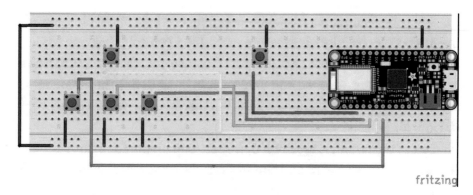

Figure 11-11. *The circuit diagram for the BLE controller*

The simplest and most accessible way to accomplish this project's circuit is to use a breadboard. We can easily place our buttons and then use wire to route it to the Feather board that can also plug directly into the breadboard with male headers, as shown in Figure 11-12 with the circuit fully assembled.

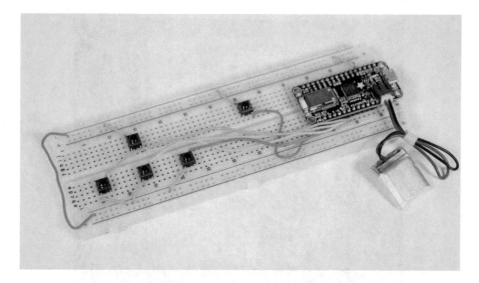

Figure 11-12. *The breadboarded BLE controller. Notice that the buttons are arranged to mimic a keyboard layout with the brake button off to the side.*

Since the Feather board can directly plug in a LiPo battery for power, the project can be fully wireless and resemble a controller's shape while still living on a solderless breadboard. Of course, more experienced users can create a more polished and final version by soldering the circuit to some protoboard and creating a case, but this iteration will certainly get the job done.

Once your circuit is assembled, we can load up the code from the Arduino IDE to the board and connect our new controller via Bluetooth to the Tinker Board.

Connecting the Bluetooth Controller to the Tinker Board

With the BLE controller powered on, either through USB or the LiPo battery, navigate to the Bluetooth options in TinkerOS that are located at the bottom-right side of the task bar, as shown in Figure 11-13.

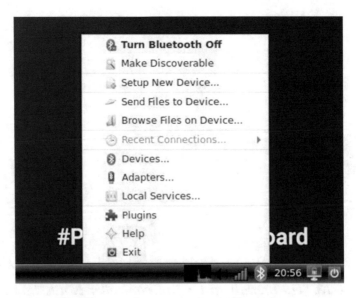

Figure 11-13. *The Bluetooth options in TinkerOS*

Select Setup a New Device from the menu, which will bring you through a setup wizard for new BLE devices. You'll be presented with a list of available BLE devices based on their MAC addresses. If you aren't sure which MAC belongs to the Feather, luckily it will show-up with a keyboard icon since it has HID properties as shown in Figure 11-14.

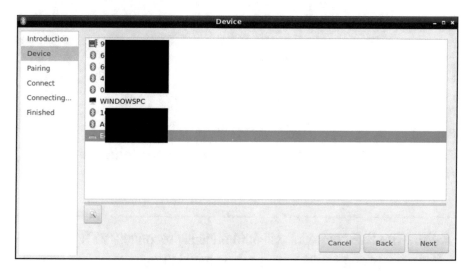

Figure 11-14. *The available BLE devices. Notice the keyboard icon for our BLE controller. The MAC addresses have been blacked out for privacy.*

After you select the device, it will take a moment to sync to the Tinker Board and then a message will pop-up to let you know it has successfully connected, as shown in Figure 11-15. You should now be able to control the roboTinker.py program via the terminal window.

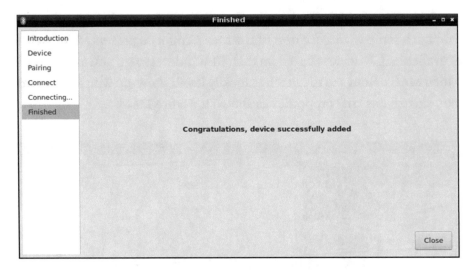

Figure 11-15. *The BLE controller has been successfully paired to the Tinker Board!*

Note   The BLE controller will automatically reconnect to TinkerOS after reboots and shutdowns, so you shouldn't have to go through this process again unless you purposely disconnect it.

Robot Assembly

Now that all the software and hardware is ready, you can take your robot chassis of choice and mount the motors, Tinker Board with the Motor HAT, camera choice, and power banks onto it so that it will resemble the one pictured in Figure 11-16.

Figure 11-16. *A fully assembled Tinker Board robot. You can go for any aesthetic you want with your assembly. If you leave the zip ties uncut like the robot in the picture, it can appear to have little antennae.*

The most important thing for this process is to ensure that everything is safely secured, both physically and electrically. To mount the Tinker Board, it's recommended to use some stand-offs so that it isn't making direct contact with any conductive surfaces, as shown in Figure 11-17. If you're using a ribbon cable camera module, make sure that it's mounted so that it will be kept safe from any static; again, these cameras can easily become damaged and as a result unusable.

Figure 11-17. *The Tinker Board mounted to a robot chassis with stand-offs*

Wire management is also very important here, since you'll want to keep your wire routing for all components neat and out of the way of any motors. Everything should be tightly secured, but not too tight; you want to avoid any strain that could cause damage over time. For the battery banks, especially the USB one used for the Tinker Board, you can use Velcro and zip ties to safely secure them and their accompanying cables.

Once everything is assembled on the chassis, you can power up the Tinker Board and Motor HAT, log in to the MJPG-stream on a browser, and begin to drive your robot around.

Final Thoughts

This project is probably the most impractical of the projects in this book; however, it's assembled with a lot of practical components ranging from Bash scripts to hardware communicating over I2C and even a custom BLE controller. Hopefully this and all the previous chapters have given you the tools to not only get started with the Tinker Board, but truly explore it and use it confidently.

Index

© Liz Clark 2019
L. Clark, *Practical Tinker Board*, https://doi.org/10.1007/978-1-4842-3826-4

S

T

Y, Z

Printed in the United States
By Bookmasters